"This book will meet a real need for the many [parents] ... who long to pray their children home and experience God's peace while they're waiting."

—**Cheri Fuller**, speaker and author of *Mother-Daughter Duet* and
The One Year Women's Friendship Devotional

"I am thrilled that this book has been written. Parents of prodigals need so much encouragement to keep praying even when they don't see any evidence of the answer."

—**Fern Nichols**, founder and president of
Moms In Touch International

"Years of pastoring and counseling have brought many parents my way who have wayward children. Our God, who answers prayer, is the key in children returning to God and to their parents. I look forward to using this resource to help many hurting parents!"

—**Dr. Kerry L. Skinner**, KLS/Life Change Ministries

"My mother, Ruth Bell Graham, would have loved this book *Prayers for Prodigals*. Why? Because she loved prodigals; I know—I was one. James Banks certainly captures the hearts of many mothers and fathers who agonize over wayward children. Even for children who don't walk the prodigal path, all children, teenagers, and adult children need prayer. This book puts such prayer into proper perspective—James has shared from the depth of experience the secret of parental prayers for children and reveals the truth for effective prayer—God's Word. He looks inward first to his own shortfall so that God can then lead him to touch the heart of a loving heavenly Father as he seeks the mind of Christ. I believe if every parent would peruse these pages they would find guidance and comfort in trusting the Lord with their dearest possessions."

—**Franklin Graham**, president and CEO of
Billy Graham Evangelistic Association and Samaritan's Purse

"As a father and grandfather, I have sometimes searched hard for words to express both gratitude and longing for our young ones. I find James Banks's words of prayer honest and helpful, and have already shared them with my grown children for their own use!"

—**Leighton Ford**, president of Leighton Ford Ministries

PRAYERS

for

PRODIGALS

90 DAYS OF PRAYER FOR YOUR CHILD

JAMES BANKS

Discovery House®
from Our Daily Bread Ministries

Prayers for Prodigals
© 2011 by James Banks
All rights reserved.

Discovery House is affiliated with Our Daily Bread Ministries, Grand Rapids, Michigan.

Requests for permission to quote from this book should be directed to:
Permissions Department, Discovery House, P.O. Box 3566,
Grand Rapids, MI 49501, or contact us by e-mail at permissionsdept@dhp.org

To protect the privacy of the persons portrayed in this book,
some names have been changed.

Library of Congress Cataloging-in-Publication Data

Banks, James, 1961-
    Prayers for prodigals : 90 days of prayer for your child / James Banks.
       p. cm. ————————————
    Includes bibliographical references.
    ISBN 978-1-57293-452-8
    1. Parents—Prayers and devotions. 2. Bible—Devotional literature.
3. Problem children. I. Title.
    BV4845.B35 2010
    242'.645—dc22   2010045045

Printed in the United States of America

Fifth printing in 2015

I have no greater joy than to hear that
my children are walking in the truth.
3 JOHN 1:4

To my children, with faith, hope, and love.

CONTENTS

Week 13: God's Timing (Mark 5:36)   217

ACKNOWLEDGEMENTS

God gives us people along the way who help make writing books easier and also help with the challenges of parenting prodigals. I've needed *both*, and I'm deeply thankful for all of them.

Annette Gysen, Judith Markham, Carol Holquist, and Katy Pent, your vision for this book has been such a blessing! Miranda Gardner, your careful editing and heart for God's Word are an answer to prayer! What a joy it is to work with each of you!

I'm especially thankful for the praying people of Peace Church in Durham, North Carolina: Ken and Barbara Davis, Bob and Marty Griffin, John and Janet Northing, Wendy Watson, Bruce and Jan Gray, and Richard and Betsy Hamilton (and many others!). You have shown me the Savior.

Don Westbrook, Junius Westbrook, Dub Karriker, Dick Bigelow, Mac Bayer, Scott McClintock, and Wade Bowick, your faithfulness in prayer is changing our city, and it has given me strength and comfort time and again.

Dave Wineman, Frank Carter, David Beaty, Howard and Margaret Shockley, and Dick and Shirilee Little, your wisdom and compassion in challenging seasons have been a gift from God. Bob Mayer, Joel Collier, Garth Roselle, Ed McCallum, John Holecek, and Alan Wright, your encouragement has helped keep me going! Sister Damian and Sister Cam and Kathy from the Avila Center in Durham, you opened a "Bethany" place of rest for me for writing and praying. May God bless you for it!

Cari, you're not only my beautiful wife of twenty-five years, you're also the most amazing mother I've ever seen. This book would not have happened without you.

All praise belongs to the one true God, my Savior—Father, Son, and Holy Spirit—who give life and breath and every hope and blessing. Soli Deo Gloria!

INTRODUCTION

Prodigals are not limited in gender, race, age or color. They do have one thing in common: They have left home, and they are missed.

RUTH BELL GRAHAM

When you have a prodigal child, prayer doesn't always come easily. You know you *need* to pray, but you don't know where to begin. That's why this book was written.

God blessed me with two prodigals. I use the word *blessed* because they are a gift, just like every child. Prodigals are an especially precious gift because they teach us much, including patience, the depth of our own need for forgiveness, and continual dependence on God in prayer. When our children bring us to our knees, we're in the best position for God to help us.

Some of God's best lessons are His most challenging. When we come to the end of our own strength, we learn to rely on His. Through prayer He takes us by the hand and leads us to fresh places of grace that we never would have seen if the challenges had not come.

Prayers for Prodigals will help you pray and remind you of the power of God to answer prayer for your prodigal child. Ninety Scripture-based prayers, one for each day of the week, cover many of the emotional and practical challenges faced by the parents of prodigals. Each week begins with a brief meditation that includes personal stories or examples of how God has moved in the lives of prodigals in the past, and most importantly, inspiration from the life and promises of Jesus. Some of the prayers are written for a son and some for a daughter, but they will work for either if you change the pronouns as you pray.

I hope you will use the prayers as a starting point for your own prayers. That's why an "amen" hasn't been added to most of them. I hope you'll add thoughts of your own and keep praying in Jesus' name for your child's salvation. Space has been provided at the end of each prayer for you to write your thoughts as you bring the specific needs of your child before God.

Besides praying on your own, I suggest gathering others to pray with you as well. A husband and wife praying for their child make a powerful team. Some parents choose a particular hour of the night to pray for their child, and let their child know that they are praying at that time. Some choose a day to fast together, or ask others to intercede daily with them for specific needs in their child's life. Praying for a son or daughter at a prayer meeting as Jim Cymbala did (see Week 5, "The Stretcher of Faith") can open the door for God to move in your child's life in a beautiful way.

You'll find further encouragement for prayer at my website PrayersForProdigals.org. If you have a testimony of how God has moved in your prodigal's life in answer to praying through this book, please share it with me!

It is my heartfelt prayer that God will use this book to change your child's eternal future, and through *your* prayers bring your son or daughter into a vital relationship with Jesus. Nothing in this world or the next could possibly matter more.

Don't Cry

*When the Lord saw her, his heart went
out to her and he said, "Don't cry."*

LUKE 7:13

Ruth and Billy Graham knew well the struggles of parenting a prodigal. In her book *Prodigals and Those Who Love Them,* Ruth tells of waking up worried in the middle of the night:

> It was early in the morning in another country. Exhausted as I was, I awoke around three o'clock. The name of someone I loved dearly flashed into my mind. It was like an electric shock.
>
> Instantly I was wide awake. I knew there would be no more sleep for me for the rest of the night. So I lay there and prayed for the one who was trying hard to run from God. When it is dark and the imagination runs wild, there are fears only a mother can understand.
>
> Suddenly the Lord said to me, "Quit studying the problems and start studying the promises."
>
> Now, God has never spoken to me audibly, but there is no mistaking when He speaks. So I turned on the light, got out my Bible, and the first verses that came to me were Philippians 4:6–7: "Be careful for nothing; but in every thing by prayer and supplication *with thanksgiving* let your requests be made known unto God. And the peace of God, which passeth all understanding, shall keep your hearts and minds through Christ Jesus" (italics Graham's). Suddenly I realized the missing ingredient in my prayers had been "with thanksgiving." So I put down my Bible and spent time worshiping Him for

who and what He is. This covers more territory than any mortal can comprehend. Even contemplating what little we do know dissolves doubts, reinforces faith, and restores joy.[1]

Sometimes we have to purposefully choose Jesus when it may be the last thing we "feel" like doing. Peace and confidence come when we drop our distractions and focus on Jesus alone, because "he himself is our peace" (Ephesians 2:14). When nerves are raw, emotions tense, and schedules overwhelming, we *need* to go to our rooms, "close the door and pray" (Matthew 6:6). We have to drop everything and spend time with God, remembering that He is "majestic in holiness, awesome in glory, working wonders" (Exodus 15:11). As we do, He will meet us in our place of need.

The New Testament tells of how Jesus was entering the gates of "a town called Nain" when he encountered a large funeral procession for the only son of a widow. Luke carefully points out that "when the Lord saw her, his heart went out to her and he said, 'Don't cry.'" Then Jesus reached out, "touched the coffin," and *stopped* the procession. He spoke to the young man and raised him from the dead. Then Jesus "gave him back to his mother" (Luke 7:11–15).

The word Luke uses to describe Jesus' heart going out to the mother implies a depth of compassion from the center of His being (literally, His "gut"). When we weep over our own children, we can rest assured our Savior's heart goes out to us in the same way. He longs to comfort us and help us as He alone can.

But for that to happen, sometimes we have to wait for Jesus. We have to allow Him to *stop* us in what we're doing. Then we need to place what we're facing in His hands. The woman had no idea what Jesus was about to do. What He did defied logic and changed *everything*.

The funeral procession became a party. Luke writes, "They were all filled with awe and praised God" (7:16). Weeping turned into worship, and despair into delight. All because of Jesus. He had brought them unexpected joy.

Before Jesus stopped the procession that day, they had no idea who He was. But *we* do. We already know Him as "the Christ, the

---

1. Graham, *Prodigals and Those Who Love Them*, 50–51.

Son of the living God," always worthy of worship (Matthew 16:16). He is "the resurrection and the life" (John 11:25), who will give life to our kids.

Knowing that, we can stop putting one foot in front of the other and wait for him.

He is coming our way.

And He has something to say to our sons and our daughters.

Come ye sinners, poor and needy
Weak and wounded, sick and sore;
Jesus ready stands to save you,
Full of pity, love and power.

JOSEPH HART, "COME, YE SINNERS,
POOR AND NEEDY"

Eternal Encouragement

*May our Lord Jesus Christ himself and God our
Father, who loved us and by his grace gave us eternal
encouragement and good hope, encourage your hearts
and strengthen you in every good deed and word.*

2 THESSALONIANS 2:16–17

"Eternal encouragement."
I *love* those words, Father.
"Eternal encouragement *and* good hope."
I really need both right now.
Not just for me, but for my child.
He is far from you and needs to come home,
    and he needs me to pray.
He needs me to pray now more than ever before,
    and you alone can help me to do that.
Help me to pray, Lord Jesus. I ask you to *teach* me to pray,
    like you did for the disciples (Luke 11:1).
Help me to pray every day, throughout the day.
Fill me with your Spirit and let your love flow through me into my
    child's life.
Like the widow who "kept coming" to the judge's door
    until her request was answered (Luke 18:3),
        help me to persevere in praying "day and night" (Luke 18:7)
    so that I will see real progress in my child's heart.
Jesus, you said that "everything is possible for him
    who believes" (Mark 9:23).
"I do believe; help me overcome my unbelief!" (Mark 9:24).
Save my son, Lord! I thank you in advance for what you will do to
    rescue him from "the dominion of darkness" and bring him into
    your "kingdom of light" and love (Colossians 1:12–13).
I believe that you will do this because "we live by faith,
    not by sight" (2 Corinthians 5:7).

I believe that you will do this because you have promised it.

Your Word says that "from everlasting to everlasting the LORD's love is with those who fear him, and his righteousness with their children's children" (Psalm 103:17).

Thank you for the eternal encouragement you alone can give.

I am encouraged! You are God, and you answer prayer!

Your "love never fails" (1 Corinthians 13:8)!

You have brought my own prodigal heart home,

and I thank you that you will do the same for my child.

"I love you, O LORD, my strength" (Psalm 18:1), and I praise you for the day when my child will love you too!

When You Feel Like a
Failure as a Parent

*To him who is able to keep you from falling and to present you before
his glorious presence without fault and with great joy . . .*

JUDE 24

I don't know how many times I've felt like there must have been
    something more I could have done as a parent, Father.
If I had just had more of your love, strength, and wisdom, perhaps
    my child would have made choices that would have kept her
    close to you.
I would have changed some things if I had known then
    what I know now.
Forgive me, Father, where I "have sinned" and
    fallen "short of" your best (Romans 3:23).
Because I can't change what has already happened,
    I pray that you will open my heart to new things you are doing,
    so that I "do not dwell on the past" (Isaiah 43:18).
Help me instead to "press on toward the goal to win the prize
    for which God has called me heavenward in Christ Jesus"
    (Philippians 3:14).
You've told me that "my grace is sufficient for you,
    for my power is made perfect in weakness" (2 Corinthians 12:9).
Thank you for reminding me that I must depend on you, Father,
    and that you are able to present me before you
    "without fault and with great joy."
Help me to be "very careful" how I live,
    "not as unwise, but as wise."
Help me to make "the most of every opportunity" to point my daughter
    to you with consistency and sincerity (Ephesians 5:15–16).
Because you give "grace to the humble" (Proverbs 3:34),
    help me to set an example in everything I do,
    just as you have done for me (John 13:15).

Help me to keep my eyes "fixed on you, O Sovereign LORD"
(Psalm 141:8) so that I will not rely on myself or my own strength
but be strong in you, in your "mighty power" (Ephesians 6:10).
Where I have my blind sides, Father, "forgive my hidden faults"
(Psalm 19:12).
Let nothing about me be a "stumbling block" (Romans 14:13).
Help me to let my "light shine" before my daughter, Lord, so that
she may see the good I do and praise you for it (Matthew 5:16).
Direct my heart into your "love and Christ's perseverance"
(2 Thessalonians 3:5).
Holy Spirit, let me "be filled with" you (Ephesians 5:18)
so that "streams of living water will flow from within" me
(John 7:38), "welling up to eternal life" (John 4:14).
Not just for me, but for the child I love.

David, Goliath, and the
Name of the Lord

David said to the Philistine, "You come against me with sword and spear and javelin, but I come against you in the name of the LORD Almighty, the God of the armies of Israel, whom you have defied."

1 SAMUEL 17:45

Sometimes encountering the rebellion in my child's life
    feels like I'm facing a giant, Lord.
We're up against so much that it's hard to know where to begin.
So instead of sizing up the giant, I'd rather keep my eyes on you.
You are the commander of "the armies of heaven" (Revelation 19:14).
Nothing can stand against you!
Like David when he faced Goliath, it is "in the name of the LORD
    Almighty" that I take my stand.
Only your power can win this battle, because "our struggle is not
    against flesh and blood, but against the rulers, against the
    authorities, against the powers of this dark world and against the
    spiritual forces of evil in the heavenly realms" (Ephesians 6:12).
The struggle is not with my child, but with the spiritual forces
    that influence him to turn away from you.
I come against the 'giant of rebellion' in my child's life in the name
    of "the LORD, strong and mighty, the LORD mighty in battle"
    (Psalm 24:8).
Because you are "the LORD who strikes the blow" (Ezekiel 7:9),
    I pray that you will use every means to cause the giant to fall.
This isn't about my will in his life. It's about yours.
I ask that you, "the Holy One" who has no equal (Isaiah 40:25),
    will come between my child and anything that could cause him
    harm.
I pray that "through the unfailing love of the Most High he will not be
    shaken," but only drawn closer to you (Psalm 21:7).

Then he will know you as "the LORD Our Righteousness"
(Jeremiah 33:16).
Because you are "the LORD, who heals" (Exodus 15:26),
I pray you will restore his relationship with you in every way,
that he may be eternally blessed.
Thank you that "it is not by strength that one prevails" (1 Samuel 2:9),
but only through your grace and awesome power to answer prayer!
I praise you, Father, that the giant of rebellion is very small compared
to you.
It is in the invincible name of the Father, and the Son, and the Holy
Spirit that I lift this prayer with love to you.

Casting Cares

Cast all your anxiety on him because he cares for you.

1 Peter 5:7

How do you do it, Lord?
You're able to take all of the cares of the world on your shoulders,
    including my cares for my child.
You're able to carry them continually!
Not only do you carry them, you're also able do something about them.
How amazing you are! Thank you for caring for me and my child.
"You, O God, are strong," and "you, O Lord, are loving"
    (Psalm 62:11–12).
I come to you today to cast all my cares on you.
More than anything else, I ask that my daughter will "come to know"
    you, Lord Jesus (Ephesians 4:20).
I long for her to have a living relationship with you.
    If she walked with you, how blessed she would be!
I cast this care and ask that your Spirit draw her to you.
I pray she will repent and turn to you and prove her repentance
    by the things she does (Acts 26:20).
I'm also concerned for her safety, Lord. The choices she's made and
    the friends she's chosen have frequently put her in harm's way.
I know only part of it. But you know all of it.
Only you can keep her safe, Lord, though I try too.
Your "forces are beyond number,"
    and those under your command are "mighty" (Joel 2:11).
Please send your angels to watch over her.
May your "power and might" protect her, Lord (Jeremiah 16:21).
I cast this care and place her in your arms again.
    There's no better place for her to be.
I also lift her future to you, Father.
I pray she will seek your kingdom with her heart, mind, and strength
    and work for what pleases you.

I pray that you will be in her and she in you (John 17:23)
    so that she will have the joy of knowing you "face to face"
    (1 Corinthians 13:12)!
Until that day, I pray that your "divine power" will give her
    everything she needs "for life and godliness" (2 Peter 1:3).
You have given us such "very great and precious promises," Lord
    (2 Peter 1:4)!
I praise you that the weight of my cares, no matter how heavy they
    may seem to me, are light to you and easy for you to carry.
"Praise be to the Lord, to God our Savior,
    who daily bears our burdens" (Psalm 68:19).
I cast *all* my cares upon you!

A Place for Anger
(in God's Hands)

*My dear brothers, take note of this: Everyone should be quick
to listen, slow to speak and slow to become angry, for man's anger
does not bring about the righteous life that God desires.*

JAMES 1:19–20

Father, one of the harder challenges I face with my child is what to do
when I am angry.

I want to be careful not to discipline him while unrighteously angry,
because that will give him cause to resent what I've done and
rebel all the more.

Your Word tells me, "do not embitter your children, or
they will become discouraged" (Colossians 3:21).

Today I ask that you will help me to be "slow to speak
and slow to become angry" (James 1:19).

Give me grace to "follow the way of love" (1 Corinthians 14:1).

With that as my aim, I'm going to practice 'counting to ten' and
placing my anger in your hands.

One. I acknowledge that "man's anger does not bring about the
righteous life" that you desire, especially when it comes to my
son's life. Show me your way, Lord.

Two. Let me follow your wisdom and not sin (Psalm 4:4) when I
cannot avoid being angry.

Three. Help me to search my heart and "be silent" (Psalm 4:4),
waiting for your Spirit to lead me, because "the mind controlled
by the Spirit is life and peace" (Romans 8:6).

Four. Make me "quick to listen" (James 1:19). Help me to respond
and not react, so I will not jump to conclusions or make hasty
decisions that I will regret later.

Five. Help me to keep my head "in all situations" (2 Timothy 4:5),
so that I may have wisdom to direct my son in the way he
should go.

Six. When the time comes to discipline my son, fill me with an extra measure of love for him, because "he who loves" his son "is careful to discipline him" (Proverbs 13:24).

Seven. Give me grace to be careful with my words, so that even when I am angry I will say "only what is helpful for building others up according to their needs, that it may benefit those who listen" (Ephesians 4:29).

Eight. Once I have disciplined my son, help me to "restore him gently" (Galatians 6:1), and to remind him of how much we both love him.

Nine. Help me to "not let the sun go down" while I am angry (Ephesians 4:26), so that I will not harbor any resentment in my heart for anything he has done.

Ten. Please give me grace to "pray continually" (1 Thessalonians 5:17), so that I may place my son and myself in your hands moment by moment.

Then together we will walk from a season of anger
into a season of your blessing and joy.

On Your Shoulders

O Sovereign Lord, my strong deliverer . . .

Psalm 140:7

I remember when he was little and he loved to have me
    carry him on my shoulders.
He felt bigger there—taller, stronger, able to face anything.
He felt safe and secure.
I can't carry him anymore, Lord. Not like that.
But I'm reminded of your Word: "The one the Lord loves
    rests between his shoulders" (Deuteronomy 33:12).
Father, I ask that you pick him up and carry him.
You are our "strong deliverer" (Psalm 140:7)!
I praise you that we face no situation that is greater than you.
I'm reminded of what Moses told Israel: "You saw how the Lord your
    God carried you, as a father carries his son" (Deuteronomy 1:31).
Father, my son needs you to carry him now.
I pray he will recognize his own limitations and understand his need
    for you.
Help him to humble himself before you,
    so that you will lift him up (James 4:10).
Give him grace to understand how your
    "power is made perfect in weakness" (2 Corinthians 12:9).
Let him hear you say, "Even to your old age and gray hairs I am he,
    I am he who will sustain you. I have made you
    and I will carry you" (Isaiah 46:4).
You have carried me, Father, again and again.
I praise you for all the times you've given me hope,
    just what I needed at just the right moment.
Because "you, O God, are strong" and "you, O Lord, are loving"
    (Psalm 62:11–12), I thank you that you will move in my son's life
    in answer to this prayer.

I pray my son will long to spend time with you
and know the comfort you give to those who love you.
I look forward to the day he will say, "My soul finds rest in God alone;
my salvation comes from him" (Psalm 62:1).
Just as you told your people in the wilderness, "I carried you on
eagles' wings and brought you to myself" (Exodus 19:4),
bring him out of the wilderness that he's in
and let him "see your face" (Psalm 17:15)!
I look forward to the day that you will "lift up" his head (Psalm 3:3).
And on that wonderful day he will see all the way from here
to eternity!

In the Shadow of Your Wing

Because you are my help, I sing in the shadow of your wings.

PSALM 63:7

How good it is just to take a moment with you, Lord!
Thank you for your faithfulness to me and my child.
Just like Jacob, "I am unworthy of all the kindness and faithfulness
    you have shown," Father (Genesis 32:10).
You are always there, the one who watches over us (Psalm 121:5).
You have been so good to us! How can I not praise you?
"I will praise you, O Lord my God, with all of my heart"
    (Psalm 86:12).
"I will praise the LORD, who counsels me" (Psalm 16:7).
"I will praise you as long as I live" (Psalm 63:4).
"I will praise you more and more" (Psalm 71:14).
Thank you that you can even give me grace to praise you
    in difficult places.
When challenges come, I "find refuge
    in the shadow of your wings" (Psalm 36:7).
When you give and when you take away,
    "may the name of the LORD be praised" (Job 1:21).
"Why should I fear when evil days come" (Psalm 49:5)?
You are "the faithful God" (Deuteronomy 7:9).
Help me to offer "a sacrifice of praise" to you (Hebrews 13:15).
There's no better place than the "shadow of your wings,"
    and no better love than your "faithful love" (Isaiah 55:3).
No matter how difficult the day, I praise you that it will not last,
    because "you guide me with your counsel,
    and afterward you will take me into glory" (Psalm 73:24).
I pray for the grace to praise you every day, because you always
    deserve it.
Help me to say with David, "I will extol the LORD at all times;
    his praise will always be on my lips" (Psalm 34:1).

You "give peace at all times and in every way" (2 Thessalonians 3:16).
You are "my strength" (Exodus 15:2), "my joy and my delight"
    (Psalm 43:4), "my Lord and my God" (John 20:28).
"O Sovereign Lord, my strong deliverer" (Psalm 140:7), because your
    mercy extends "from generation to generation" (Luke 1:50),
    I ask that my daughter will one day know your love
    and take refuge in you as well.
Then "I will praise you forever for what you have done" (Psalm 52:9).
Better still, together "we will praise your name forever" (Psalm 44:8)!

The Power of a Parent's Prayers

People were bringing little children to Jesus to have him touch them,
but the disciples rebuked them. When Jesus saw this, he was indignant.
He said to them, "Let the little children come to me, and do not hinder
them, for the kingdom of God belongs to such as these."

MARK 10:13–14

When you're the parent of a prodigal child, you're sometimes the recipient of unsolicited advice. When our daughter ran away at the age of fifteen, one well-meaning professional advised us to "let her fall flat on her face."

"After all," he continued, "kids have to learn from their own mistakes."

Some of that advice is sound. There are lessons our children have to learn for themselves that we cannot teach them, try as we may. But the day we found our daughter and brought her home (against her will), she had been befriended by another teenage runaway with an adult boyfriend fresh out of jail. They were encouraging her to leave the state with them. Letting her "fall flat on her face" would have been a dangerous thing to do.

It may be difficult for other parents to understand *exactly* what you're up against with a prodigal son or daughter, especially if they haven't walked the same road with their own children. But God understands. He knows what it's like to have a world full of prodigals. And he waits for us to bring *ours* to Him through committed, passionate prayer.

Prayer combined with a believing mother's or father's love is powerful. When placed in Jesus' hands, it is invincible. Obstacles may come when you least expect them, but perseverance in prayer will lead to a breakthrough. Our God is the "One who breaks open the way" (Micah 2:13). Jesus was *indignant* with the disciples for creating an obstacle when they rebuked parents for bringing their children to Him for His blessing. "Let the little children come to me," he said (Mark 10:13–14). *Indignant* is used nowhere else in the New Testament to describe how Jesus felt about something, and it sets apart His passion for our children and how much He wants to bless them.

We must do whatever it takes to bring our prodigals to Jesus in prayer, because Jesus wants to bless us and our children through our prayers. The world's perspective is that a "blessed" child is one who grows up to be happy, well-adjusted, and successful in a career. But even "successful" kids can be prodigals, and Christian parents who have them have to be careful not to be lulled into a false sense of security. God has given us our children for eternal purposes, and there is no greater blessing and inheritance we can pass on to them than our prayers for their salvation.

Most importantly, we are blessed to have a Savior who longs for our children to come to Him! Let others say what they will. We have *His* promises, and that is all that matters. Remember what the Pharisees and teaches of the law muttered about *Jesus*? "This man welcomes sinners and eats with them" (Luke 15:2).

There's a place in His heart for prodigals. Especially *our* prodigals as we bring them before Him in prayer.

My mother's prayers! Oh, my sweet, blessed mother's prayers. Did ever a boy have such a mother as I had? For twenty five years I have not heard her pray, till tonight I have heard all her prayers over again.

TESTIMONY OF A MAN WHO CAME TO CHRIST DURING THE 1857–59 PRAYER MEETING REVIVAL, YEARS AFTER HIS MOTHER'S DEATH

When You Can't Change the Consequences of His Actions

The king covered his face and cried aloud, "O my son Absalom!
O Absalom, my son, my son!"

2 Samuel 19:4

I remember when my son was little, Father,
    and his problems were so much easier to fix.
A skinned knee, a lost toy, a flat tire on his bike—those were things
    I could more or less handle.
That has changed now.
He faces problems that I would love to make go away,
    but it's no longer in my power to do that.
Now he has to face the consequences of his actions,
    and it isn't easy, for him or for me.
I can't imagine how David felt when he faced his son's rebellion,
    but David's words stay with me: "Be gentle with the young man . . .
    for my sake" (2 Samuel 18:5).
I ask for my son what David asked for his, Father:
    Please "be gentle with the young man."
I thank you that I don't ask this of mere men, as David did.
I ask it of the One who "has compassion on all he has made"
    (Psalm 145:9).
You are "rich in mercy" (Ephesians 2:4),
    and I'm grateful for the mercy you have for my son, Lord.
I understand that if he does not face the consequences of his actions,
    he may not learn from them.
But I would rather have him fall into your hands, for your
    "mercy is great," than "into the hands of men" (2 Samuel 24:14).
That is why I place his circumstances into your hands,
    and ask that you bless him as you alone can.

You have told me, "as the heavens are higher than the earth,
 so are my ways higher than your ways
 and my thoughts than your thoughts" (Isaiah 55:9).
You see the best way through his problems, Father!
I pray you will bring good from them
 that could not have come about any other way.
I love you, Lord, and praise you that "in all things" you are at work
 "for the good of those who love" you (Romans 8:28).
I pray that my son will love you too!
Use *all of this* to turn his heart to you, because that is what matters most.
I pray that he will come to you to "have life, and have it
 to the full" (John 10:10).
If he has that, he has all he will ever need.

The Son of These Tears

*Even now my witness is in heaven; my
advocate is on high. My intercessor is my
friend as my eyes pour out tears to God.*

JOB 16:19–20

"It is not possible that the son of these tears should perish."[1]
Those words spoken to a mother centuries ago as she prayed for her
  son encourage me too, Lord.
Not only did you save her son, Augustine,[2]
  but you used him to bring many others to you!
Lord Jesus, I thank you that I am not the only one praying for my son.
I praise you that you are "interceding for us" in
  heaven (Romans 8:34)!
How blessed I am that "my intercessor is my friend" (Job 16:20).
Even my tears matter to you. You keep track of every one—
  "are they not in your record?" (Psalm 56:8).
Thank you, Father, that there is hope for 'the son of these tears.'
You promise in your Word that "those who sow in tears will reap
  with songs of joy" (Psalm 126:5).
Thank you that I may 'reap a harvest' in my son's life as I pray for him!
Lord Jesus, just as you "offered up prayers and petitions with loud
  cries and tears" and were heard because of your "reverent
  submission" (Hebrews 5:7), help me to pray with passion and
  commitment, and to "pray continually" (1 Thessalonians 5:17).
I believe one reason you've given my son to me is so I can pray for him
  to have the joy of knowing you forever.

---

1. Augustine, *Confessions*, 3.12, available at http://www.ccel.org/ccel/augustine/ confess.iv.xii.html.
2. God would use Augustine's faith to inspire generations to believe in Jesus. He became the most influential theologian in the early centuries of the church, and his influence is still felt today. For more about Augustine's early life, see Week 13, "God's Timing."

Praying for him is one of the greatest purposes of my life, and I don't
   want to miss it. Most of all, I don't want *him* to miss *you*!
Help him understand that you are "gracious and compassionate,"
      and that you will not turn your face from him
      if he returns to you (2 Chronicles 30:9).
I pray he will know the riches of your "kindness, tolerance and
      patience" (Romans 2:4), and be filled "with your unfailing
      love" (Psalm 90:14).
Your "love endures forever" (1 Chronicles 16:34). We will not have
      enough time, even with eternal life, to give you all the love
      you deserve.
I praise you for the day you will "wipe away the tears from all faces"
      (Isaiah 25:8), even from the face of 'the son of these tears'!
Then we will "weep no more" because you will be our joy (Isaiah 30:19),
      and we will worship you, "King of the ages" (Revelation 15:3),
      through every age to come!

Bring the Boy to Me

"O unbelieving generation," Jesus replied, "how long shall I stay with you? How long shall I put up with you? Bring the boy to me."

MARK 9:19

Here he is, Lord.
This is my son, and he needs you desperately.
I bring him to you, all that he is and all that is going on in his life.
His life is beyond my power to repair or set right.
I ask you to touch him and help him, Lord!
Years ago when you told the disciples, "Bring the boy to me,"
 you began the greatest blessing of the child's life.
Darkness had to flee. It could not stand in your presence.
 So I bring my son into "the light of your presence"
 again today (Psalm 89:15).
I'm reminded of what you told your disciples.
 The child could be set free "only by prayer" (Mark 9:29).
The disciples had tried everything they could think of,
 but no matter how hard they tried in their own strength,
 "they could not" make any difference (Mark 9:18).
You rebuked them for their lack of faith. Then you said,
 "Everything is possible for him who believes" (Mark 9:23).
I'm beginning to understand how much I need to bring my son to you
 in faithful, believing prayer.
He needs the difference only you can make for him.
How wonderful that father must have felt when he walked away with
 his son, happy and healthy and standing strong.
He had brought his son to you, and you freed the boy!
Lord Jesus, I look forward to that day in my son's life as well,
 the day he meets you and is transformed by your love,
 rescued "from the dominion of darkness," and brought
 "into the kingdom of the Son" (Colossians 1:13).
What a day that will be!

There will be "rejoicing in heaven" (Luke 15:7) and if I'm still here, on earth as well!

By faith I see it coming, and I pray that day will come soon.

I believe you will save my son, and that nothing will stand in your way!

I look forward to that moment when "the day dawns and the morning star rises" in his heart (2 Peter 1:19).

Please, Lord, could that day be today?

The Plans You Have

"For I know the plans I have for you," declares the LORD,
"plans to prosper you and not to harm you,
plans to give you hope and a future."

JEREMIAH 29:11

I want your plans for my child, Lord, not mine.
My plans still have too much of the world in them: this school, that
    career path, that success . . .
Forgive me, Father, because too many times I have had in mind
    not "the things of God, but the things of men" (Mark 8:33).
I ask that you lift my eyes to a more lasting vision, Father.
Your plans for my child would take my breath away!
 "How precious to me are your thoughts, O God!" (Psalm 139:17).
Your thoughts are "too wonderful for me to know" (Job 42:3).
Your plan for my child is perfect
    and magnificently exceeds the scope of my vision.
May "your will be done" in her life, Father (Matthew 6:10)!
Today I ask for eternal things for my daughter.
I ask that she will be someone "after" your "own heart"
    (1 Samuel 13:14), who makes you her "trust, who does not look to
    the proud" (Psalm 40:4) or the ways of this world.
I pray that she "may live a life worthy of" you "and may please" you
    "in every way: bearing fruit in every good work, growing in the
    knowledge of" all that you are, "being strengthened with all
    power according to" your "glorious might" (Colossians 1:10–11).
Just as "all the days ordained for" her "were written in your book
    before one of them came to be" (Psalm 139:16), I pray that you
    will use even this season of rebellion in her life for eternal
    purposes.
Once she turns "from the error of" her way (James 5:20), I ask that
    she will "lead many to righteousness" (Daniel 12:3).

"You can do all things," Lord! "No plan of yours can be thwarted" (Job 42:2).

Because "all things hold together" in you (Colossians 1:17),
I ask that you hold her together when she seems to be falling apart.

Help her discover your plans and purposes for her life and love you for them!

I pray that you will prosper my daughter not only in this world, but especially in the world to come.

May you be her hope and her future (Jeremiah 29:11), because you "have the supremacy" in everything (Colossians 1:18)!

Restored

*He prays to God and finds favor with him, he sees God's face and
shouts for joy; he is restored by God to his righteous state.*

JOB 33:26

"He prays to God and finds favor with him,
> he sees God's face and shouts for joy; he is restored . . ."
I can see my son in this verse! This is exactly what I want for him!
There is no joy like the joy you give.
There is nothing better than being restored to a right relationship
> with you.
I long to see my son wearing "a garment of praise instead of a spirit of
> despair."
I long to see him standing firm in you, an oak "of righteousness,
> a planting of the LORD for the display of his splendor" (Isaiah 61:3).
The oak may be in winter now, and much seems barren.
But spring will come! I pray he will turn his heart to you and
> "grow in the grace and knowledge" of all that you are
> (2 Peter 3:18).
You gave this child to me so I could raise him to believe in you.
You brought him from my body and placed him in my arms
> so I could pray for him to know you and love you for all eternity.
I have prayed for him, even before he was born,
> and now I will "not give up" praying for him (Galatians 6:9).
Today I "live by faith, not by sight" (2 Corinthians 5:7)
> as I wait for him to turn to you.
But "I am still confident of this: I will see the goodness of the LORD in
> the land of the living."
I will "be strong and take heart and wait for the LORD"
> (Psalm 27:13–14).
Seasons change! And this one will. The darkness will pass.
I stand on your truth: "The LORD is God,
> and he has made his light shine upon us" (Psalm 118:27).

"Shine forth" (Psalm 80:1), Father!
Let your light overcome any darkness in his life!
"All things are possible" with you (Mark 10:27)!
"Restore us, O LORD God Almighty;
   make your face shine upon us, that we may be saved" (Psalm 80:19).
By faith I see your face shining on my son,
   and him looking back at you, his face radiant with joy.
May "everlasting joy" be ours, Father (Isaiah 61:7)! His, mine, and
   yours! To your glory, now and forever!

The Difference Prayer Makes

The prayer of a righteous man is powerful and effective.

JAMES 5:16

Father, I praise you for the privilege of prayer.
You have answered my prayers so many times in so many ways!
Even when the answer wasn't what I was looking for at the time,
    you've shown me repeatedly that your "wisdom is profound"
    (Job 9:4).
Thank you that because of Jesus I may "approach the throne of grace
    with confidence," so that I may "receive mercy and find grace"
    in my "time of need" (Hebrews 4:16).
I have not earned the privilege of approaching the throne in prayer. I
    do not deserve it. You allow me to do so because of *your* goodness.
Your Word tells me that the prayers of a righteous man
    are powerful and effective—and this means that even *my* prayers
    are, because of what you have done for me.
Jesus has become for me my "righteousness, holiness and redemption"
    (1 Corinthians 1:30).
I can't thank you for that enough!
So I come to you again, Father, praising you that
    "Jesus came into the world to save sinners" (1 Timothy 1:15),
    and asking for your help for my daughter.
I praise you that my prayers can make a difference.
    You answer prayer! You choose to work through our prayers.
You promise to "give good gifts to those who ask" (Matthew 7:11).
Forgive me, Father, for my lack of faith,
    and the times I've wondered if it really matters if I pray.
How could you not answer prayer?
You are "the compassionate and gracious God, slow to anger,
    abounding in love and faithfulness, maintaining love to
    thousands, and forgiving wickedness, rebellion and sin"
    (Exodus 34:6–7).

I praise you that you "hear when I call" on you
> for my prodigal child (Psalm 4:3).

You are "my hope" and "my confidence" (Psalm 71:5).

I praise you that my prayers can change history,
> because "all things are possible" with you (Mark 10:27).

So here she is, Father, the child you blessed me with,
> a gift from your hand and your heart.

I pray that you will save her in absolutely every way imaginable!

And I praise you that you are "able to do immeasurably more than all"
> I "ask or imagine" (Ephesians 3:20), because you are "the great,
> mighty and awesome God" (Nehemiah 9:32)!

If I Should Die before She Wakes
(I Pray the Lord Her Soul to Take)

All these people were still living by faith when they died.
They did not receive the things promised; they only
saw them and welcomed them from a distance.

Hebrews 11:13

Father, I want so much to see my daughter come to you.
    But what if it takes longer than my lifetime?
I will still live by faith,
    and welcome your answer to my prayers "from a distance."
I'm amazed by how you treasure prayer, Father.
You keep our prayers before you in "golden bowls" (Revelation 5:8),
    rising like incense.
Because you hold our prayers in your heart, you can even add years to
    them that exceed our lives on earth.
How amazing you are, Father!
I come to you in faith again for my precious daughter.
Even if she doesn't come to you during my time on this earth,
    I praise you that you will still be at work to answer my prayers
    for her salvation.
How I long to see her soul awaken to you, Lord! To life, abundant
    (John 10:10), eternal (John 3:15), and free (Revelation 22:17)!
I'm reminded of your Word: "Wake up, O sleeper, rise from the dead,
    and Christ will shine on you" (Ephesians 5:14).
Shine on her, Lord! Make your light shine in her heart to give her
    "the light of the knowledge of the glory of God in the face of
    Christ" (2 Corinthians 4:6).
Speak life to her, Lord, just like you did to Jairus' daughter
    (Luke 8:54).
Not a life that will end in death someday, but one that will "never die"
    (John 11:26)!

Call her out of sin's deadly payback (Romans 6:23), into the kindness you have "prepared for those who love" you (1 Corinthians 2:9).

If I should die before she wakes, let me be standing near when you say to her in heaven, "Well done, good and faithful servant . . . Come and share your master's happiness!" (Matthew 25:23).

Oh, that her life may be lived for the praise of your glory, Lord Jesus (Ephesians 1:12)!

This is my prayer, and I offer it with faith and hope and love, because "I know that my Redeemer lives" (Job 19:25).

I pray that she will know this too, Father.

And I praise you that *this* prayer lives on, because you do!

Wanting What God Wants

*Then the mother of Zebedee's sons came to Jesus with
her sons and, kneeling down, asked a favor of him.*

MATTHEW 20:20

Ask most parents what they want for their child and you'll find
they want good things: a successful career, a happy home, good
health, a life with fewer challenges than they've had . . .

But what does God want?

Sometimes we don't give that question as much thought as we
should. We naturally assume that God wants the "good things" we
envision for our children, and that our dreams for them are the same
as His.

That's how the mother of James and John (the sons of Zebedee) saw it. Matthew writes that "the mother of Zebedee's sons came
to Jesus with her sons and, kneeling down, asked a favor of him."
When Jesus asked what she wanted, she answered, "Grant that one
of these two sons of mine may sit at your right and the other at your
left in your kingdom" (Matthew 20:21).

Why shouldn't she ask that? After all, Jesus had called her sons
the "Sons of Thunder" (Mark 3:17). They were ambitious and had
great plans for the future and for the kingdom of God. And if anyone
got in their way, like the time a Samaritan village didn't welcome
Jesus, James and John wanted "to call fire down from heaven to
destroy them" (Luke 9:54).

If anyone "had Jesus' back," it was the Sons of Thunder. But
when Mom went to talk this over with Jesus, he responded, "You
don't know what you are asking" (Matthew 20:22).

I don't want to be too hard on James and John's mother. I have
a sneaking suspicion that they put Mom up to it. After all, certainly

the strapping "Sons of Thunder" could have made Mom stand down. But they didn't. And when Jesus responded, he answered *them* directly, not her. Notice too that Matthew tells us that "when the ten heard about this, they were indignant *with the two brothers*" (Matthew 20:24). Mom doesn't get mentioned.

Still, she *did* ask. Maybe she got pulled into her sons' scheme. Any parent of a prodigal knows how easily *that* can happen. Her actions show that she loved her kids, like any good parent, and believed in them. Still, her encounter with Jesus raises a vital question: Do I want the same things for my child that God wants?

I find that if I'm not careful, I get caught up in the world's way of thinking: a successful future means the "right" schools, major, career path, and spouse. That's good as far as it goes, but it's too shortsighted when eternity comes into view. "What good is it for a man to gain the whole world, yet forfeit his soul?" (Mark 8:36). If my kids are successful heathen who look good from the world's point of view but will be separated from God for eternity, what kind of a future is *that*?

Nothing matters more than getting right with God. If I'm trying to shape their future with anything less in mind, I'm missing the mark by a mile and then some. But if I aim for what God wants, then there's always reason for hope.

When you're the parent of a prodigal child, you may feel like you have to settle for second best when it comes to the future. Maybe you've been "keeping score" with other kids his or her age, and it seems like your child is behind. Maybe your plans haven't worked out, and you're scrambling to come up with new ones. God once promised His people, "I know the plans I have for you . . . plans to prosper you and not to harm you, plans to give you hope and a future" (Jeremiah 29:11), and His heart hasn't changed.

The future He promises isn't limited to a lifespan. Not only can God open doors for our children on this earth, he can also open heaven.

Our prayer needs to be, "Father, help me to want what *you want* for my child. Help him to love you most of all!"

When that prayer is answered, then your son or daughter will be truly happy and have all that he or she needs. Not just for a few years on this earth but for every day to come, stretching on beyond forever, because "no eye has seen, no ear has heard, no mind has conceived what God has prepared for those who love him" (1 Corinthians 2:9).

Your possessions are never so safe as when you are willing to resign them, and you are never so rich as when you put all you have into the hand of God.

CHARLES HADDON SPURGEON

Open Doors

*Now God had caused the official to show favor
and sympathy to Daniel.*

DANIEL 1:9

Some of my son's choices have affected his future, Father.
The missed opportunities, denied admissions, and closed doors would
    not have been so if he had applied the gifts that you've given him.
But that doesn't mean that he's missed the greatest opportunity of his
    life.
You are that opportunity, Lord! And you can make new opportunities
    for him.
More than wanting him to seek your hand and what you can do for
    him, I want him to seek your heart.
I pray that he will not miss all that you are.
Everything this earth has to offer pales in comparison with you
    and the beauty of a loving relationship with you.
"The heavens, even the highest heaven, cannot contain you"
    (1 Kings 8:27).
I ask that you would give him grace to comprehend deeply in his soul
    that "each man's life is but a breath" (Psalm 39:5).
You promise, "I am with you to rescue you and save you"
    (Jeremiah 15:20),
    and I pray that he will take that promise to heart.
But I also ask your help for his earthly future, Lord.
I pray you will help him to "make level paths" for his feet
    and "take only ways that are firm" (Proverbs 4:26).
Just as you gave Daniel favor when his people were strangers in a
    country not their own, I ask that you will give my son wisdom to
    follow you and find your favor.
Just as you were "with Joseph and he prospered" (Genesis 39:2)
    against all odds, I pray that he will be blessed in his work.
Only you can do this, Father. And I praise you that you can!

Please give him favor with employers and gatekeepers in a way that he will see your hand at work, and thank you for it.

Let doors open as he turns to you, so that he sees that "blessed is the man who trusts in the LORD, whose confidence is in him" (Jeremiah 17:7).

Please bless my son, Father!

Bless him with "a future hope" (Proverbs 23:18).

Bless him with "longing for your salvation" (Psalm 119:81).

Bless him with yourself!

The Way Out

*No temptation has seized you except what is common to man.
And God is faithful; he will not let you be tempted beyond
what you can bear. But when you are tempted, he will also
provide a way out so that you can stand up under it.*

1 CORINTHIANS 10:13

She's had too many close calls lately, Lord.
The hot breath of temptation has been closing in and breathing down
    her neck.
She has walked into the situations willingly,
    knowing you'd have her take another path,
    and her feet "almost slipped" (Psalm 73:2).
I ask that your "power may rest on" her (2 Corinthians 12:9),
    so that she may "choose what pleases" you (Isaiah 56:4).
I pray you will give her *your* strength, Lord Jesus, so that she may
    have all that she needs to stand strong in this challenging time
    (2 Corinthians 9:8).
I thank you that she faces no temptation that you do not understand,
    because you were "tempted in every way, just as we are,"
    yet you were "without sin" (Hebrews 4:15).
I praise you that you are able "to sympathize with our weaknesses"
    in every way (Hebrews 4:15)!
Father, I cannot praise you enough for your promise that you will
    never let her "be tempted beyond what" she "can bear."
Each time, you will provide "a way out" (1 Corinthians 10:13).
Show her the way out, Lord! Mark it with a sign so big that she can't
    miss it! Better yet, stand right beside it and call her name.
"Who will rescue" her "from this body of death?" (Romans 7:24).
You will, Lord Jesus! And I love you for it.
Lord, *you* are the way out!
You are "the way and the truth and the life" (John 14:6).
You are the "living hope" that she needs (1 Peter 1:3)!

Help her to "resist the devil" so that "he will flee from" her (James 4:7).
Restore her faith, Father, and make her
    "strong, firm and steadfast" (1 Peter 5:10).
I praise you that you are continually faithful!
I praise you that your love will never fail her or me!
Your "salvation will last forever"
    and your "righteousness will never fail" (Isaiah 51:6)!
I place my trust in you today for both myself and my daughter,
    and I ask that your grace will set her free from temptation and sin.

For Open Eyes

*I pray also that the eyes of your heart may be enlightened in
order that you may know the hope to which he has called you,
the riches of his glorious inheritance in the saints, and his
incomparably great power for us who believe.*

EPHESIANS 1:18–19

He needs to see things in a new way, Father.
He needs a new and lasting vision for his life, and only you can give
    him that.
Father, I pray that "the eyes" of his "heart may be enlightened, in
    order that" he "may know the hope" that comes from you alone.
May he know hope, and know you!
I pray that you, "the God of hope," will fill him "with all joy and
    peace" as he trusts in you, so that he may "overflow with hope by
    the power of the Holy Spirit."
Bring him to a new place in his life, Lord! A place where he is "joyful
    in hope, patient in affliction, faithful in prayer" (Romans 12:12–13).
What a future awaits him when he turns to you!
Lord Jesus, you said, "The eye is the lamp of the body. If your eyes are
    good, your whole body will be full of light" (Matthew 6:22).
I long to see you shining through his eyes!
I long to hear your Word come from his mouth,
    and to see you moving through his heart and hands.
That is the reason he was born, to know you and love you.
You "made us for this very purpose" (2 Corinthians 5:5)!
I pray he will "be made new in the attitude" of his mind,
    and that he will "put on the new self, created to be like" you
    "in true righteousness and holiness" (Ephesians 4:23–24).
Help him to understand that we are your "workmanship,
    created in Christ Jesus to do good works,"
    which you "prepared in advance for us to do" (Ephesians 2:10).
His future is wide open with you, Lord!

You hold the future in your hands, and every blessing along with it.

Help him to understand that if he is on your side, he will have all he
needs, because "there is no wisdom, no insight, no plan that can
succeed against" you (Proverbs 21:30).

Everything that the devil has used to harm him will come to nothing,
because "the reason the Son of God appeared was to
destroy the devil's work" (1 John 3:8).

"O Lord, open his eyes that he may see" (2 Kings 6:17)
and choose to follow you today!

Father, Forgive

When they came to the place called the Skull, there they crucified him,
along with the criminals—one on his right, the other on his left. Jesus
said, "Father, forgive them, for they do not know what they are doing."
And they divided up his clothes by casting lots.

Luke 23:33–34

No one is more forgiving than you, Lord. You are absolutely amazing!
After all you had suffered from our cruel hands,
    you even forgave us for torturing you.
Nothing can compare with your love. Nothing comes close.
What's more amazing is that *you* have *come close* to us!
You came near to show us how much you love us.
You died to set us free "from the law of sin and death" (Romans 8:2)
    and rose to give us life.
And while you were dying, you interceded with the Father for your
    murderers.
They really *didn't know* what they were doing, did they?
If they had understood, "they would not have crucified the
    Lord of glory" (1 Corinthians 2:8).
Thank you for your mercy, Lord Jesus. "I do not deserve" it (Luke 7:6),
    and I praise you for it.
There is such comfort in your love,
    such "tenderness and compassion" (Philippians 2:1).
You long for us with affection (Philippians 1:8),
    and my daughter really needs your compassion and affection now.
She's young and doesn't understand the consequences of her actions.
If she'd only catch a glimpse of how wonderful you are,
    then she couldn't help loving you!
Forgive her, Father. She does not know what she is doing (Luke 23:34).
I know that she must ask forgiveness for herself, and I pray that
    she will!

I understand that "no one can say, 'Jesus is Lord,'
except by the Holy Spirit" (1 Corinthians 12:3).
So I ask that your Spirit will make your "light shine" in her heart
(2 Corinthians 4:6) and give her a fresh understanding of all
that you are.
Open her eyes, Lord Jesus, and show her "the way of peace"
(Isaiah 59:8).
One day "we must all appear before" your "judgment seat"
(2 Corinthians 5:10), and I pray she will be ready!
Help me to help her in any way that I can.
Just as I was "at one time disobedient" to you and "have now received
mercy" (Romans 11:30), "may your mercy come quickly to meet"
her as well (Psalm 79:8)!
Then, together we will tell how much you have done for us
(Mark 5:19), so that others may know your mercy too!

God of the Second Chance

When they had finished eating, Jesus said to Simon Peter,
"Simon son of John, do you truly love me more than these?"
"Yes, Lord," he said, "you know that I love you."
Jesus said, "Feed my lambs."

JOHN 21:15

I love what you did for Peter, Lord.
After he had denied you three times (Matthew 26:34),
    you still forgave him and gave him another chance.
Thank you for your mercy, Lord!
Not only did you give Peter another chance, but you also gave one to me.
And you continue to give me chances. You forgive me again and again.
My son needs your forgiveness too, Lord.
He needs the second chance that only you can give him.
You said, "You must be born again" (John 3:7),
    and I pray that he would be!
Make his "calling and election sure" (2 Peter 1:10).
Let there be no doubt in his mind that you have saved him and called
    him "to a holy life—not because of anything we have done,"
    but because of your "purpose and grace" (2 Timothy 1:9).
Father, I praise you that you want "*all men* to be saved
    and to come to a knowledge of the truth" (1 Timothy 2:4).
That includes my son!
I thank you that you want him to be saved and have placed the desire
    in my heart to pray for him.
I pray for a second chance for my son, just like you gave Peter.
I ask you, "Lord of the harvest," to "send out workers" into the
    "harvest field" (Matthew 9:38) that is my son's life.
Let him encounter your people wherever he goes,
    and let them share your love with him in ways he cannot miss.
Let his heart be "burning within" (Luke 24:32)
    when he encounters you speaking to him through your people.

Then open his eyes so that he may recognize you and turn his heart to
you again.

Lord Jesus, you promised that "whoever comes to me I will never
drive away" (John 6:37).

I pray he will come to you today!

New Mercy!

Because of the LORD's great love we are not consumed,
for his compassions never fail. They are new every morning;
great is your faithfulness.

LAMENTATIONS 3:22–23

Something good is coming, and I thank you for it,
    even though I don't know what it is yet!
But I know *you*, and your kindness is "new every morning."
Thank you, Lord, for your kindness to me and my daughter.
Thank you that when I am tired and come to the end of my strength,
    your strength keeps me going.
"My flesh and my heart may fail,"
    but you are "the strength of my heart" forever (Psalm 73:26).
"It is good to be near" you (Psalm 73:28).
It is good to know that I can come to you with every need
    and find you ready and waiting, tirelessly able to answer prayer.
Thank you for the incredible hope that you give.
"Whom have I in heaven but you?" (Psalm 73:25).
I will not give in to fear and doubt and worry because you are with me.
You are "my helper" (Psalm 118:7),
    "my fortress and my deliverer" (2 Samuel 22:2).
I praise you that because of your "great love we are not consumed"
    (Lamentations 3:22).
You gave yourself "for us to redeem us from all wickedness"
    and to make us your "very own" (Titus 2:14).
I pray that new mercy will flow into my daughter's life with purpose
    and power so that she may find the "better hope" that will enable
    her to "draw near" to you (Hebrews 7:19).
Then together we "will exalt you and praise your name, for in perfect
    faithfulness you have done marvelous things" (Isaiah 25:1).
We will find new things to praise you for that we haven't discovered
    yet, mercies still on the way from your loving hand.

Because of your kindness, I will renew my hope in you today.
You are "good to those whose hope is in" you (Lamentations 3:25).
I plead your mercy for my daughter, Lord,
> that she may soon find her heart's desire in you.

And I praise you that that day is coming, because your "compassions
never fail." "Great is your faithfulness" (Lamentations 3:23)!

Take Heart!

I have told you these things, so that in me you
may have peace. In this world you will have trouble.
But take heart! I have overcome the world.

John 16:33

How good it is to hear you say, "take heart," Lord!
I praise you that I can "take heart" because you "have overcome the
world" and have overcome every obstacle my child and I will face.
We encounter nothing that you cannot handle!
No wonder your Word says, "Be strong and take heart,
all you who hope in the Lord" (Psalm 31:24).
My hope is in you, Lord!
I can be "greatly encouraged" because I "have this hope as an anchor
for the soul, firm and secure" (Hebrews 6:18–19).
You always live "to intercede" for us (Hebrews 7:25)!
Even now while I am praying, you are bringing my needs before the
Father.
He raised you "from the dead and seated" you "at his right hand . . .
far above all rule and authority, power and dominion, and every
title that can be given, not only in the present age but also in the
one to come" (Ephesians 1:20–21).
He "placed all things" under your feet (Ephesians 1:22),
even the troubles we face!
I praise you, Lord Jesus, because you meet our need and "save
completely those who come to God through" you (Hebrews 7:25–26).
I praise you for the promise that the Father will meet all our needs
"according to his glorious riches in" you, Jesus (Philippians 4:19)!
As I bring my son to you today, I think of what you told another
young man: "Take heart, son; your sins are forgiven" (Matthew 9:2).
I long for him to hear you say that!
I long for him to ask for the forgiveness only you can give!

Lord Jesus, I pray that you will remove anything from his path
    that keeps him from coming to you.
Give him insight that "friendship with the world" will not get him
    anywhere but further away from you (James 4:4).
Help him understand that "the world and its desires pass away,
    but the man who does the will of God lives forever" (1 John 2:17).
I want him to live forever with you, Lord,
    and I take heart today because you want him to as well!
I take heart that he may one day have peace in you as I do
    because you answer prayer.
I pray he will receive your peace today, Lord.

The Running Father

*While he was still a long way off, his father saw him
and was filled with compassion for him; he ran to his son,
threw his arms around him and kissed him.*

LUKE 15:20

Dancing eyes, a cherub's face, and a shock of dark brown hair. I remember the first time I held my son in my arms. He was born quickly, twelve minutes after we arrived at the emergency room. There wasn't even time to hook up his mom's IV.

But all was well. Our baby boy was healthy and strong and mom was doing great. Just as we had done with his sister, before we left the hospital Cari and I enjoyed a quiet moment with our best friend, John. We took our son in our arms, bowed our heads, and gave him to God.

It would be the first of many prayers on his behalf.

All children need our prayers, especially those who pass through prodigal years. Bryan's childhood was idyllic. He was affectionate and loved to spend time with his family. We took trips, played games, and read good books and God's Word together. He was in Sunday school every Sunday of his life and received Jesus as his Savior at age seven. The years were full, and his childlike faith was sincere.

Little did we know that the sunshine of that season would give way to the clouds of another.

It was after midnight when the phone rang.

"Dad, it's me."

"Are you OK, Bryan?"

"I'm fine, but I'm spending the night at Andy's."

"That's not what we agreed to. You said you'd be home by midnight."

"I know, Dad. But . . . I really shouldn't drive, and Andy can't drive me home either."

I could tell by the sound of his voice that Bryan had been drinking. While he was making the right decision by staying off the roads, he knew better than to put himself in that situation to begin with.

When your child goes through prodigal years, you wonder where you went wrong as a parent. Not only do your children question you, *you* question *yourself*. You sometimes feel as if the whole world is watching, and you wonder if anyone truly understands.

Someone does.

When we were going through a particularly challenging time with Bryan, a friend pulled me aside after a meeting at our church. "I want you to know that I pray for you and your son every day," he said. Then he added: "I feel so guilty."

"Why do you feel guilty?" I asked, puzzled.

"Because I've never had to deal with prodigal children," he confided. "My daughters pretty much played by the rules. It's only now beginning to dawn on me how fortunate I was, and it wasn't because of anything I did or didn't do. I feel as if I've been spared, somehow. Kids," he shrugged, "make their own choices."

I wanted to hug him. I distinctly felt that God sent him at that moment with an insight I deeply needed to hear. His compassion was a gift from God, communicating to me the Father's understanding for my struggle with my son.

No one understands the struggle with prodigals better than our heavenly Father. The story of the prodigal son is our story and God's. Jesus told it on behalf of all sinners who need so desperately to come home to their Creator and discover the warmth of a loving relationship with Him.

The story of the prodigal son is the ultimate search and rescue. Jesus' mission was to "seek and to save what was lost" (Luke 19:10). In the story, He paints a poignant picture of a father who does what was unthinkable for a parent in that culture at that time. Instead of standing at a distance while his son limped home, he looked for him and *ran* to him. Luke records Jesus' words: "While he was still a long way off, his father saw him and was filled with compassion for him; he ran to his son, threw his arms around him and kissed him" (Luke 15:20).

Jesus is God seeing us in the distance and looking on us with compassion. He is God running to us and throwing His arms around us. He is heaven's kiss welcoming the repenting sinner home.

No one cares more about prodigals than Jesus. Jesus *loves* my prodigal son and welcomes my prayers for him. Jesus wants to restore him to the Father and welcome him home. He has called me to join in *His* search and rescue mission. Together, we're going after my son.

Jesus loves Bryan even more than I do. He loves him so much that He died to save him. And He longs for my prayers on Bryan's behalf.

After all, I gave Bryan to Jesus on the day he was born. And Jesus said, "Let the little children come to me, and do not hinder them, for the kingdom of heaven belongs to such as these" (Matthew 19:14). How could I do anything less than pray for my son?

Even though his way is dark and Bryan is far from home, God hasn't just left the light on for him. He's out on the front porch, watching, waiting, calling. And He's asked me to join Him.

Our loved ones may spurn our appeals, reject our message,
oppose our arguments, despise our persons—
but they are helpless against our prayers.

J. Sidlow Baxter

No Record of Wrongs

Love is patient, love is kind. It does not envy, it does not boast,
it is not proud. It is not rude, it is not self-seeking,
it is not easily angered, it keeps no record of wrongs.

1 Corinthians 13:4–5

I need the reminder, Lord, that love "keeps no record of wrongs."
I don't want to be the kind of parent who holds things against his
    child. Not anything. Not ever.
I know that you told me, "if you do not forgive men their sins,
    your Father will not forgive your sins" (Matthew 6:15).
How could I not forgive? You've forgiven me everything!
"You have put all my sins behind your back" (Isaiah 38:17).
Every sin I have ever committed has been taken away
    "as far as the east is from the west" (Psalm 103:12).
Thank you, Father, for loving me with such amazing love!
The more I live, the more I understand how much I need forgiveness
    and what a precious gift it is.
My daughter needs forgiveness too.
Someday she will need to know that I've forgiven her for any wrong
    she's done, even if she doesn't understand that yet. Please help me
    to do this, Lord.
In this moment, I pray for a heart that is willing to forgive. I want her
    to experience real forgiveness, from you and from me.
I want to leave anything she's done to me at the foot of the cross.
I want to put it behind us forever, and I ask your help to never bring it
    up again.
I also ask your forgiveness, Father, for all of the times I've angrily
    reminded her of her sins and mistakes, and recounted to her
    my own personal "record of wrongs" (1 Corinthians 13:5).
Help me to have a heart like your own, Lord, "merciful and forgiving,
    even though we have rebelled" (Daniel 9:9).

I know that claiming to forgive and forget is easier said than done,
because my tendency is to hold on to wrongs done against me.
Help me, Father, to let go of those hurts.
Please give me a heart that delights in grace and mercy.
I ask for grace to stand strong when I need to discipline her,
because "better is open rebuke than hidden love" (Proverb 27:5).
I also ask for grace to "gently instruct, in the hope that" you will
grant her "repentance leading . . . to a knowledge of the truth"
(2 Timothy 2:25).
When she comes to you and repents, what a beautiful moment that
will be!
She will be like the woman who "loved much" because
"her many sins have been forgiven" (Luke 7:47).
Just like mine.
And together, we will praise you for your mercy forever!

For Perfect Love to Drive Out Fear

There is no fear in love. But perfect love drives out fear,
because fear has to do with punishment.
The one who fears is not made perfect in love.

1 JOHN 4:18

I want to be done with fear, Father.
I worry about my daughter because I love her,
    and it's hard for me not to worry.
But I know that I worry too much.
You told me not to "worry about tomorrow,
    for tomorrow will worry about itself."
You told me that "each day has enough trouble of its own"
    (Matthew 6:34).
I ask your forgiveness for borrowing trouble from tomorrow, Lord.
I know you have something far better in mind.
Help me draw near to you
    "with a sincere heart in full assurance of faith" (Hebrews 10:22).
I pray for grace to look forward to each new day, and ask that you
    fill me with "the faith and love that spring from the hope that is
    stored up for" me "in heaven" (Colossians 1:5).
I also ask that your perfect love will drive out fear from my life
    as I seek to lead my child to you.
Fill me with your love, Lord, in such a way that she sees you in me.
You are perfect love, Lord!
Help me to love her boldly and unselfishly, because you did not give
    us "a spirit of timidity, but a spirit of power, of love and of self-
    discipline" (2 Timothy 1:7).
Father, I praise you that I "did not receive a spirit that makes" me
    "a slave again to fear," but I "received the Spirit of sonship.
    And by him we cry 'Abba, Father'" (Romans 8:15)!
Abba, Father, please bless my child!

I want to say, "I sought the Lord and he answered me;
  he delivered me from all my fears" (Psalm 34:4).
Lord Jesus, I ask that your perfect love will drive out any fear
  in my daughter's heart about coming to you.
Help her understand that knowing you is all about love,
  which is so very different from any less-than-loving examples of
  legalism or judgmentalism she may have seen along the way.
I pray that your love may be "made complete" in her so that she
  "will have confidence on the day of judgment" (1 John 4:17).
Let her live in love, because "whoever lives in love lives in" you
  (1 John 4:16), and you in them.
May the wonder of all that you are bless my child
  and draw her heart to you today!

Extra Miles

If someone forces you to go one mile, go with him two miles.

MATTHEW 5:41

Sometimes I feel like I have some extra miles on me, Father.

There are days it seems like my child needs me to 'go the extra mile' more than once.

Thank you, Lord Jesus, that my child's needs are teaching me to serve him in ways that you have served me.

You "did not come to be served, but to serve,
   and to give" your life (Matthew 20:28).

I pray you will help me to serve my son in a way that will point him to you.

Help me to have your attitude, Lord.
   You took on "the very nature of a servant" (Philippians 2:7).

This isn't an easy road, but I accept it gratefully
   knowing that I'm following you.

I know by faith that this road comes out in a better place for him and for me if I keep my eyes on you.

I pray that I will continue in "faith, established and firm, not moved from the hope held out in the gospel" (Colossians 1:23).

Because love "always perseveres" (1 Corinthians 13:7),
   help me to take the steps I need to take to help my son
   "without complaining or arguing" (Philippians 2:14).

Help me to understand that "the end of a matter is better than its beginning, and patience is better than pride" (Ecclesiastes 7:8).

Your eyes "range throughout the earth to strengthen those whose hearts are fully committed to" you (2 Chronicles 16:9).

You are not only watching, you are *with me.*

When I "pass through the waters" of difficult days, you have promised, "I will be with you."

When I "pass through the rivers"—those days when we're in over our heads—you have said, "they will not sweep over" us.

Even when I "walk through the fire" of trial or temptation or anger, I "will not be burned" if I stay close to you (Isaiah 43:2).

You have promised to be with us always (Matthew 28:20)!

Help me stay close to you in such a way that my son will learn to follow.

Let me walk humbly with you, knowing that I am an "unworthy" servant, and I "have only done" my "duty" (Luke 17:10).

I ask for your unconditional love so that I can love my son like you do, Father.

May he see your love in me and love you for it, forever and ever.

For Grace to Abound at Home

And God is able to make all grace abound to you,
so that in all things at all times, having all that you need,
you will abound in every good work.

2 CORINTHIANS 9:8

Sometimes I don't feel like I have much grace, Father.
My child knows just the right 'buttons' to push,
 and sometimes even seems to enjoy pushing them.
We need more grace at home, Lord!
There's been too much tension lately. Sometimes we are so focused on
 dealing with the negative that we lose sight of positive things.
Help me to "give thanks in all circumstances,"
 because that is exactly what you want me to do
 (1 Thessalonians 5:18).
Help me to never lose sight of the truth that "the joy of the LORD" is
 my strength (Nehemiah 8:10).
I need to be filled with your joy, Father!
I don't want my son to see my faith as simply a set of 'dos and don'ts.'
I want him to see you in me!
Give me grace to grow all of the fruit of your Spirit:
 "love, joy, peace, patience, kindness, goodness,
 faithfulness, gentleness and self-control" (Galatians 5:22–23).
I pray you will also give him grace, Lord.
I trust your promise that you are "able to make all grace abound,"
 "in all things at all times."
Help me to "abound in every good work" (2 Corinthians 9:8),
 so that he may see my "good deeds and praise" you, Father
 (Matthew 5:16)!
I ask for grace to discipline him with the love and wisdom you alone
 can give so that I may show him "the way to life" (Proverbs 6:23)
 because your Word says "he who loves" is "careful to discipline"
 (Proverbs 13:24).

Help me to be careful "not to put any stumbling block or obstacle" in his way (Romans 14:13).

I praise you that from the fullness of your grace "we have received one blessing after another" (John 1:16).

I praise you that I have all that I need (2 Corinthians 9:8)!

Help me to share those blessings with my son in every way, so that your grace may be "poured out" on him "abundantly, along with the faith and love" (1 Timothy 1:14) that you alone can give!

You Promised!

But you have said, "I will surely make you prosper and will make your descendants like the sand of the sea, which cannot be counted."

GENESIS 32:12

Thank you for Jacob, Lord. He reminded you of the promises you
    made to him, and you blessed him because of it!
His boldness reminds me that you want me to pray your promises too.
Your promises build my faith and give me hope.
They help me remember your kindness and give me strength to go on.
Your Word makes it clear that your promises can be trusted:
    "God is not a man, that he should lie, nor a son of man,
    that he should change his mind. Does he speak and then not act?
    Does he promise and not fulfill?" (Numbers 23:19).
You keep your promises!
Because you are absolutely perfect, it is impossible for you to lie.
Your Word is filled with promises I want to pray again and again,
    especially for my child.
Like Jacob, I want to pray what "you have said." After all, you
    promised, Lord!
You said, "I will do whatever you ask in my name, so that the Son may
    bring glory to the Father. You may ask me for anything in my
    name, and I will do it" (John 14:13–14).
I know it would bring glory to the Father if my daughter gave her
    heart to you, so I ask in your name, Lord Jesus, that she will!
You also tell me to have faith when I pray.
You said, "Whatever you ask for in prayer, believe that you have
    received it, and it will be yours" (Mark 11:24).
I *do* believe that she will turn from the world and receive you,
    because you promise to answer prayer!
I hold on to this promise from your Word: "Believe in the Lord Jesus,
    and you will be saved—you and your household" (Acts 16:31).

I look forward to the day when everyone in my home will praise you together, Lord.

I believe this is entirely possible for you to accomplish,
and I hang on to your promise that "everything is possible for him who believes" (Mark 9:23)!

Thank you that I can rely on your Word because you are reliable.

You said about your Word, "It will not return to me empty,
but will accomplish what I desire and achieve the purpose for which I sent it" (Isaiah 55:11).

I know you've given me your Word so I can fill my heart and my life with it.

I will "trust in your word" (Psalm 119:42), and you with it!

Help me to "diligently study the Scriptures" (John 5:39)
in order to know you better and love you more.

Then I will keep finding promises to pray,
and praise you all the more when you keep them!

Thank You

Sons are a heritage from the LORD, children a reward from him.

PSALM 127:3

I don't think I've said "thank you" enough lately, Lord.
Your Word reminds me that children are a blessing from you,
    and I take that to heart.
I'd like to thank you again for the blessing of my son.
He is your own beautiful and unique creation.
There will never be anyone exactly like him.
I praise you because he is "fearfully and wonderfully made;
    your works are wonderful, I know that full well" (Psalm 139:14).
I thank you for my son's good characteristics.
I even thank you for the strength of his will and look forward to the
    day that it will be used to serve you with devotion and resolve.
I thank you for the things I sometimes take for granted:
    the blessings of health, and food, and a roof over our heads.
Even though times are challenging right now,
    I don't want to stop saying thank you.
Your Word tells me to "give thanks in all circumstances, for this is
    God's will for you in Christ Jesus" (1 Thessalonians 5:18).
I thank you especially for your patience with my son, and with me.
Help me to "bear in mind that our Lord's patience means salvation"
    (2 Peter 3:15).
Though my son hasn't turned his heart to you yet,
    I thank you that you are still waiting, still bearing with him,
    still holding out your hand.
O, Father, I pray that his salvation will come soon!
Thank you, Father, for the hope of your salvation.
    Thank you for the wonder and beauty of all that you are.
Your patience with me and my son gives me reason for hope.
Even though others may doubt you are near, I hang on to you and
    trust in you.

Thank you, Father, for the kindness you have shown us in so many
ways!
Your goodness never ends: "The things you planned for us no one can
recount to you; were I to speak and tell of them, they would be
too many to declare" (Psalm 40:5).
You are always faithful,
"a faithful God who does no wrong" (Deuteronomy 32:4).
Thank you for your promise that "though the mountains be shaken
and the hills be removed, yet my unfailing love for you will not be
shaken" (Isaiah 54:10).
"How priceless is your unfailing love!" (Psalm 36:7).
I thank you for the blessing of a child whom I dearly love, Lord,
and praise you that you love him even more than I do.
"Show us your unfailing love, O LORD,
and grant us your salvation" (Psalm 85:7).

Blessed without Knowing It

When Jacob awoke from his sleep, he thought, "Surely the LORD
is in this place, and I was not aware of it."

GENESIS 28:16

You never cease to surprise me, Lord.

There have been many times when you were at work in my son's life,
and I didn't know it.

I'd like to thank you for those times, Father, especially for the ones
that are happening right now that I'm unaware of.

You told Nicodemus, "The wind blows wherever it pleases. You hear
its sound, but you cannot tell where it comes from or where it is
going. So it is with everyone born of the Spirit" (John 3:8).

You are at work in ways that I may not see for years.

Nothing escapes you—you have heard my prayers for my son and are
lovingly responding.

Your faithfulness makes me want to pray all the more.

I praise you that you never stop working, Lord.

You "will not grow tired or weary,"
and "no one can fathom" your understanding (Isaiah 40:28).

It helps to remember that when I'm feeling worn out!

My son can run from you only so long, because "even youths grow
tired and weary, and young men stumble and fall" (Isaiah 40:30).

Catch him, Lord! Be there when he falls to his knees and calls out
to you.

I thank you that you will be there to lift him up and hold him close,
just like I used to do when he fell as a boy.

"Speak tenderly" to him that his sin "has been paid for" (Isaiah 40:2),
and lead him home to you.

You have ways to reach him that I have not thought of, Father.

You do "great things beyond our understanding" (Job 37:5).

How many blessings have I not thought of?

How wonderful you are, Lord! "How great is your goodness, which you have stored up for those who fear you" (Psalm 31:19)!

Just like Jacob, who realized that your presence surrounded him, I pray you will awaken my son to the beauty of your presence.

Let him hear you say, "I am with you and will watch over you wherever you go" (Genesis 28:15).

As you did with me, bring him to the understanding that your blessing reaches further than he could ever imagine, and let him praise you for it forever.

The Stretcher of Faith

When Jesus saw their faith, he said to the paralytic,
"Son, your sins are forgiven."

MARK 2:5

My mother had the spiritual gift of faith (1 Corinthians 12). When I was a teenager, few things bothered me more.

"Just trust God," she'd tell me. "He will take care of you." Sometimes she'd smile and break into song, finishing her thoughts with a hymn.

It used to drive me up a wall. I can still hear my protests as I'd stomp off: "It isn't that simple, Mom!"

But to her it was. She knew God was faithful. He had always taken care of her. During the Great Depression when her father died young and through the Second World War and the Korean War when Dad was frequently in harm's way, Mom held on to faith, and God held on to her.

Mom suffered from Alzheimer's disease in her final years. Dad had cared for her until he died, and then she came to live with Cari and me until she needed additional care. There were blessings in those days we never saw coming. Though Mom had forgotten much, the hymns she so dearly loved remained. Sometimes I'd sing to her and she'd remember the words with surprising clarity and join in.

At the time of Dad's death, the family agreed to sell Dad and Mom's home to fund Mom's extended care needs. Dad had bought the house fully furnished as part of an estate sale when I was in seventh grade, and because Mom was facing an illness that would last for several years and money was limited, all of the contents of the house would be appraised and sold.

Once again, God came through for Mom. At the appraisal, two paintings were discovered. They were the work of Granville Redmond, a California Impressionist artist. Together they sold at auction for more than four hundred thousand dollars, funding Mom's care to the end of her days.

Even when Alzheimer's assaulted her mind and her memory, God showed His faithfulness to her through those paintings in a way that I would never forget. It *changed* me. Sometimes I can hear my mother's own words coming out of my mouth to my own children: "Just trust God. He will take care of you."

Faith must be caught as well as taught. Parents of prodigal kids need to pray that their faith will be evident to their children. Children need to catch their parents actively believing and see their parents' faith lived out.

Mark and Luke tell a striking story of Jesus "catching people in the act" of faith. Four men brought a friend who was paralyzed to Jesus for healing. When they couldn't find a way through the crowd, they climbed up on the roof of the home where Jesus was teaching, removed some tiles, and lowered the man "right in front of Jesus" (Luke 5:19). Mark and Luke both write that "when Jesus saw *their* faith," he healed their friend (Mark 2:5, Luke 5:20).

Notice that both Mark and Luke mention more than just the faith of the man who was healed. Jesus saw "*their* faith," indicating the faith of his friends. When the man was paralyzed and could do little for himself, the active faith of those around him made all the difference.

When we pray for our prodigal kids, we carry them on stretchers of faith to Jesus. We do the heavy lifting, but they receive the benefit. They may be entirely passive or even actively resisting us, but Jesus sees *our* faith as we bring them to Him.

Jim Cymbala writes of his daughter Chrissy's return after a long prodigal season.[1] One Tuesday evening, God moved the church he serves (The Brooklyn Tabernacle) to intercede passionately for his daughter. He came home that evening and told his wife, "It's over with Chrissy. You would have had to be in the prayer meeting

---

1. Cymbala, *Fresh Wind, Fresh Fire*, 64–65.

tonight. I tell you, if there's a God in heaven, this whole nightmare is finally over."

Two days later, his daughter came home to her family and back to God. She asked one question over and over: "Daddy . . . *who was praying for me? Who was praying for me?*"

That Tuesday night God moved in her soul and showed her she was headed toward destruction, all the while affirming His love for her. Somehow she *knew* He had used the passionate prayers of His people to bring her back to Him.

Our prodigal kids desperately need us to lift them to Jesus on the stretcher of prayer. Even if they don't have faith, He will see ours. And *they* will be blessed because of it.

The great battle of our spiritual lives is "Will you believe?" It is not, "Will you try harder?" or "Can you make yourself Worthy?" It is squarely a matter of believing that God will do what only he can do.

JIM CYMBALA

Snatched from the Fire

Be merciful to those who doubt;
snatch others from the fire and save them.

JUDE 22–23

He's been playing with fire, Lord, and he doesn't even know it.
He thinks he's having 'a good time' doing whatever he wants to do.
He doesn't realize that "there is a way that seems right to a man,
> but in the end it leads to death" (Proverbs 14:12).
Father, the thought of my son being anywhere near the vicinity of
> "the fire of hell" (Matthew 18:9) is almost too painful for me
> to bear.
But because I am shielded by your power (1 Peter 1:5),
> I will face that fear and go after him with this prayer.
I ask that you will use me in any way you want to save my son.
> Whatever it takes, Lord!
God, help me to snatch him "from the fire."
I can't do it on my own. But "I can do everything through him
> who gives me strength" (Philippians 4:13)!
Thank you that I'm not alone in this, Lord. I am depending on your
> strength.
We're going after him together, because you are
> "with me like a mighty warrior" (Jeremiah 20:11).
The foes we face may be many.
But I remember what your people prayed in a past battle:
> "We do not know what to do, but our eyes are upon you"
> (2 Chronicles 20:12).
I look to you for my son's salvation, and for you to overcome every foe.
Rebuke the adversary, Lord (Zechariah 3:2)!
Your Word says that the children of believers "are holy"
> (1 Corinthians 7:14).

I know my son still must turn to you to be saved, but I also know that
the adversary steps onto holy ground to pursue my son
and takes aim at someone whom both of us love.

Lord Jesus, when Peter confessed, "You are the Christ, the Son of the
living God" (Matthew 16:16), you replied that "the gates of Hades
will not overcome" that confession (Matthew 16:18).

I confess you as Lord as well!

Break down those gates, Lord! Pull my son from the fire while there is
still time!

I pray that my son will repent of his sins
and confess you as his Lord and Savior today.

May today be the time of your favor.

May today be "the day of salvation" (2 Corinthians 6:2)!

A Softer Heart

I will give you a new heart and put a new spirit in you;
I will remove from you your heart of stone and give you
a heart of flesh. And I will put my Spirit in you.

EZEKIEL 36:26–27

Lord, I've read how you "hardened the heart of Pharaoh"
    (Exodus 14:8) to set your people free.
Since you hardened his heart to bless your people,
    may I ask you to soften my son's?
You promise in your Word,
    "I will give you a new heart and put a new spirit in you."
What a blessing that would be for my son!
I pray you will move in his heart today in a fresh and powerful way.
His heart has been "hardened by sin's deceitfulness" (Hebrews 3:13),
    but it wasn't always that way.
There was a time when he was open to you. He received you
    and your love was at work in him in a beautiful way.
But his faith has been "choked" by this world (Luke 8:7).
"Life's worries, riches and pleasures" have led him astray
    and held him back from growing strong in you (Luke 8:14).
"But with you there is forgiveness" (Psalm 130:4).
There is still hope for him, and I praise you for it!
Just as Solomon prayed that you would turn the Israelites' hearts to
    you (1 Kings 8:58), may you turn my son's heart to you as well!
I pray he will no longer "waver between two opinions" (1 Kings 18:21)
    but love you wholeheartedly.
When he turns to you, I know you will welcome him, because that is
    your heart!
Give him "an undivided heart and put a new spirit" in him
    (Ezekiel 11:19).
"Remove from" him his "heart of stone and give" him
    "a heart of flesh" (Ezekiel 36:27).

Then let your grace be with his spirit, Lord Jesus (Philemon 1:25), and may he know that "your Name is near" (Psalm 75:1).

May he trust that you will "never leave us nor forsake us" (1 Kings 8:57).

I pray that he will walk in all your ways, to love you and to serve you with all his heart and with all his soul (Deuteronomy 10:12).

Let his heart be "steadfast, O God" (Psalm 57:7).

Let each new day bring him hope of "your unfailing love" (Psalm 143:8).

His heart is in your hands, Father, and so is mine.

I long to see him filled with your love, Lord, and I know that you do too.

I pray that he will give his heart to you today!

Whoever

For God so loved the world that he gave his one and only Son, that whoever believes in him shall not perish but have eternal life.

JOHN 3:16

"Whoever."
Thank you for including that word in John 3:16, Lord. I love what
  it means.
It tells me that regardless of what we have done, if we come to you and
  "confess our sins," you are "faithful and just and will forgive us
  our sins and purify us from all unrighteousness" (1 John 1:9).
That means that my child can find forgiveness.
Even though others may write her off for the things she's done,
  if she turns to you, you will receive her. That is all that matters.
"Whoever"! That word gives me so much hope.
I praise you, Lord Jesus, for what you have done for us.
  Because of "the joy set before" you, you "endured the cross,
  scorning its shame, and sat down at the right hand of
  the throne of God" (Hebrews 12:2).
Does that mean that *we* are part of that joy? It must!
You said that the reason you came was
  "to seek and to save what was lost" (Luke 19:10).
You also said that if we obediently follow you,
  your "joy may be in" us, and our "joy may be complete"
  (John 15:11).
I want my daughter to know your joy so much, Lord!
  There's nothing like knowing you.
I pray she will come to understand that she has an emptiness within
  her that only you can fill.
She tries to fill it with pleasures and distractions,
  but they only leave her looking for more.
Father, I ask today that you will show her again how much you
  love her.

You love her so much that you gave your "one and only Son"!

Break through her distractions and show her the pointlessness
of going her own way and living apart from you.

Remind her that whoever does will "perish" because "the wages of
sin is death, but the gift of God is eternal life in Christ Jesus"
(Romans 6:23).

I pray for life for my daughter, Lord!

Use this prayer in your 'search and rescue mission' to pull her up to
the safety of your love. And use *me*, Father, any way you desire.

I know that you've given my daughter to me for this reason—
not only for the personal, earthly blessing of being a parent,
but because you want to use me for the salvation of her eternal
soul.

No matter what she's done, you still love her with an amazing love,
and I thank you that you will respond to every prayer for her "out
of the goodness of your love" (Psalm 69:16).

A Better Attitude

*You were taught, with regard to your former way of life, to put off
your old self, which is being corrupted by its deceitful desires; to be
made new in the attitude of your minds; and to put on the new self,
created to be like God in true righteousness and holiness.*

EPHESIANS 4:22–24

When she looks in the mirror, Father, what does she see?
Does she see only what's on the outside? Help her to take a deeper
    look, Lord.
Give her grace to look beyond her physical reflection and into
    her heart.
She needs a new attitude, Lord. She needs the encouragement that can
    come only from "faith and hope" in you (1 Peter 1:21).
I pray you will help her to "put off" her old self,
    "which is being corrupted by its deceitful desires,"
    and bloom into the person you long for her to be.
Give her a 'makeover' on the inside, Lord!
Let her be "made new in the attitude" of her mind,
    so that she looks forward to life in a way that she never
    has before.
Help her understand that with your power and love at work in her
    heart and mind, her "new self" will be the person you intended
    her to be all along, "created to be like" you.
I praise you, Father, that you love my daughter,
    and that you love her too much to leave her just as she is.
You want her to be transformed into your likeness (2 Corinthians 3:18),
    a daughter of the "King of glory" (Psalm 24:10)!
Let there be no doubt as to the family resemblance:
    may everything about her remind others of you!
Thank you, Jesus, that you were made like us "in every way"
    (Hebrews 2:17), so that we could be made like you.

Thank you, Lord Jesus, that you shared in our humanity
so that by your death you would destroy "him who holds the power of death . . . and free those who all their lives were held in slavery" (Hebrews 2:14–15).

Set my daughter free, Lord!

Free to love you, and free to live!

Free to repent of her sins and make a brand new beginning.

Free to reach her full potential and be a blessing to others.

Free to one day run barefoot in the New Jerusalem (Revelation 21:2),
because she was "born again" in you (John 3:3)!

Friends, and a Friend

A man of many companions may come to ruin,
but there is a friend who sticks closer than a brother.

PROVERBS 18:24

I pray for my son, Lord. He needs wisdom in choosing his friends.
He needs good friends, Father. Friends who know you and have a
  sincere faith, who will be faithful to you and to him, and who
  will "reject the wrong and choose the right" (Isaiah 7:15).
I pray you will protect him from friends who would lead him astray,
  because "bad company corrupts good character"
  (1 Corinthians 15:33).
Give my son the strength to "not go along with them" (Proverbs 1:15).
I ask for friends who will be attracted to his good qualities,
  and who will encourage him to develop them.
I ask for friends who will love "whatever is true, whatever is noble,
  whatever is right, whatever is pure, whatever is lovely,
  whatever is admirable" (Philippians 4:8).
You know he has friends I don't care for, Father. But I also know that
  you love them, no matter how far from you they may be.
So I pray for my son's friends who need to know you.
Save them, Lord! And let the work of your Spirit in their lives
  draw my son's heart to you as well.
You are the "friend who sticks closer than a brother."
You have promised "I will never leave you nor forsake you"
  (Joshua 1:5).
You have said, "I have made you and I will carry you;
  I will sustain you and I will rescue you" (Isaiah 46:4).
He needs rescuing, Lord, and you alone can do that.
Help him understand that he needs a friend like you most of all,
  and to turn to you with all his heart.
Thank you for being my friend, Father.
  "Your love is better than life" (Psalm 63:3).

"Because you are my help, I sing in the shadow of your wings"
(Psalm 63:7).
I look forward to what you will do in my son's life
and in the lives of his friends.
"I will praise you forever for what you have done" (Psalm 52:9),
because you "heard my cry for mercy when I called to you for
help" (Psalm 31:22).
"Great is your faithfulness" (Lamentations 3:23)!

Innocence Found

"Come now, let us reason together," says the LORD. "Though
your sins are like scarlet, they shall be as white as snow;
though they are red as crimson, they shall be like wool."

ISAIAH 1:18

I praise you, Lord, because you are innocence found.
You are "the Lamb of God, who takes away the sin of the world!"
    (John 1:29).
You are the "lamb without blemish" (1 Peter 1:19).
Your "works are perfect," and all your "ways are just."
    You are "a faithful God who does no wrong" (Deuteronomy 32:4).
You are sinlessness and wisdom together, absolute perfection!
Lord Jesus, how you could be "tempted in every way, just as we are,"
    yet be "without sin" (Hebrews 4:15) amazes me
    and makes me want to worship you all the more.
You are not only entirely sinless, you restore innocence to us because
    you are "able to save completely those who come to God through"
    you (Hebrews 7:25).
My daughter needs to be saved completely, Lord.
She needs the gift of your forgiveness and the washing away of
    her guilt.
No one can remove sin's stain like you so that we may be
    "set free from sin" (Romans 6:22) and "born again" (1 Peter 1:23)
    to a completely new life!
You promise, "Though your sins are like scarlet,
    they shall be as white as snow."
Father, I pray that you and my daughter will "reason together"
    and that she will long for the innocence that you freely give.
May she ask and find your full forgiveness.
Deep in her spirit, let her hear you say, "I, even I, am he who blots out
    your transgressions, for my own sake, and remembers your sins
    no more" (Isaiah 43:25).

Let her "escape the corruption in the world caused by evil desires"
   (2 Peter 1:4), and be "washed," "sanctified," and "justified in
   the name of the Lord Jesus Christ and by the Spirit"
   (1 Corinthians 6:11).

Through your Spirit, let her hear in her heart the hope that you have
   for her: "Forget the former things; do not dwell on the past.
   See, I am doing a new thing!" (Isaiah 43:18–19).

You are the God of new beginnings!

You can set her feet on a new path!

"The crooked roads shall become straight,"
   and "the rough ways smooth" (Luke 3:5)! Make it so, Lord!

Let her be part of the bride of Christ, "without stain or wrinkle
   or any other blemish, but holy and blameless" in every way
   (Ephesians 5:27)!

Loving Father, may your gift of innocence be hers today!

Praise because You've Been There

As he approached Jerusalem and saw the city, he wept over it
and said, "If you, even you, had only known on this day what
would bring you peace—but now it is hidden from your eyes.

LUKE 19:41–42

You've been there, haven't you, Lord Jesus?
You know what it's like to look with longing on those you love,
    hoping and praying that they will turn their hearts to the Father.
You wept over Jerusalem more than once, didn't you?
On another day you looked over the city and said, "I have longed to
    gather your children together, as a hen gathers her chicks under
    her wings, but you were not willing" (Matthew 23:37).
You "reared children and brought them up,
    but they have rebelled against" you (Isaiah 1:2).
My heart goes out to you, Lord. You know exactly how I feel
    about my son.
 "All my longings lie open before you, O Lord;
    my sighing is not hidden from you" (Psalm 38:9).
    I want such good things for him!
I long for him to see you as you are,
    and to know your joy deep in his heart.
I long for him to find the peace that only you can give.
But just like Jerusalem, at the moment "it is hidden from" his eyes.
If I have such longing about one child,
    I can only begin to imagine how you feel about an entire city!
You understand completely what is like to have a prodigal child.
Some people cannot understand because they haven't had a
    prodigal child.
I've felt the condemnation of their glances
    and the weight of the words they do not say.
Thank you, Father, that you are not that way.

You know what it's like to have a world full of prodigal children,
and only one child who did what was right—your Son, our Savior!
You love us so much, you "gave him up for us all" (Romans 8:32)!
I praise you that you did not send your "Son into the world to
condemn the world, but to save the world through him" (John 3:17).
Thank you for not looking on my son with condemnation but
with love.
You long for him to come to you just as you longed for the people
of Jerusalem.
You long for him to come to you with a depth I cannot begin
to fathom.
I pray that he will, Lord, for your sake and for his.
I pray he will understand that "now is the time" of your favor,
"now is the day of salvation" (2 Corinthians 6:2),
and give his heart fully and freely to you!

Just Say the Word

When Jesus had entered Capernaum, a centurion came to him, asking for help. "Lord," he said, "my servant lies at home paralyzed and in terrible suffering." Jesus said to him, "I will go and heal him." The centurion replied, "Lord, I do not deserve to have you come under my roof. But just say the word, and my servant will be healed . . ." When Jesus heard this, he was astonished and said to those following him, "I tell you the truth, I have not found anyone in Israel with such great faith . . ." Then Jesus said to the centurion, "Go! It will be done just as you believed it would." And his servant was healed at that very hour.

MATTHEW 8:5–13

When we were in high school, one of my older brothers made a decision he would regret. He decided to try streaking.

One sunny Saturday afternoon when Mom was quietly reading, he summoned his twin and me to the front door. Wearing only a towel, he explained his plan carefully.

"I'm going to streak out to the curb, and you guys keep watch for Mom. After I count to three, you run to the other door and make sure I don't come in that way if she's close by. Got it?"

His twin and I nodded our heads in agreement: "OK!"

"One . . . two . . . three . . . NOW!"

The towel dropped.

He bounded out the door.

And we *locked* it behind him.

We didn't only lock *that* door. While he was enjoying his "nature walk," we locked every door to the house. Within a minute, he was back and trying to open a bolted door.

The pounding on the door that followed sounded like something out of a biblical parable. But all the noise just made matters worse. It made his brothers yell all the louder, "MOM, SOMEBODY'S AT THE DOOR!"

Mom *did* answer the door. But my brother was never grounded for his misadventure. After she stopped laughing, I think she felt that the punishment already given had met the crime.

Sometimes our kids trust the wrong people and it gets them in trouble. But we find a beautiful example of who *can* be trusted in the story of the centurion with the sick servant (Matthew 8:5–13).

Moments after Jesus entered Capernaum, "a centurion came to him, asking for help" (Matthew 8:5). His servant was deathly ill, paralyzed and suffering. Immediately Jesus promised, "I will go and heal him" (Matthew 8:7).

The centurion's response was amazing: "Lord, I do not deserve to have you come under my roof. But just say the word, and my servant will be healed" (Matthew 8:8).

The centurion, charged with the responsibility of at least a hundred soldiers under his command, was used to giving orders. He represented Caesar's authority over the province where he served, and disobedience to him was the same as defying the emperor.

He saw the same kind of authority in Jesus. Only Jesus' authority came from God, and the centurion knew it. That's why he said, "I do not deserve to have you come under my roof."

There are only two incidents in Scripture where Jesus is described as being "astonished" or "amazed" (the other is with the people in his hometown in Mark 6:6). Both instances had to do with faith. In his hometown, it was the *lack* of faith that amazed him and kept him from performing miracles.

Here was a Gentile, a man representing an occupying foreign army. But he believed that Jesus could do what he promised from a distance: "Just say the word, and my servant will be healed."

That kind of faith evoked an amazing response from Jesus: "Go! It will be done just as you believed it would."

Something happened here that we must not miss. Instead of doing what He originally said He would do, Jesus did what the man *believed* He could do. And Matthew writes that "his servant was healed at that very hour" (Matthew 8:13).

What do you believe that Jesus can do for your prodigal son or daughter? It's easy to become discouraged and allow our circumstances to shape our faith (or our lack of it). But what if we take the centurion's experience of Jesus to heart? What if we believe all the more in the greatness and power of our Savior? Just a word from Him can change our prodigal's life forever.

What if we trust Jesus *more*, and believe that He is "able to do immeasurably more than all we ask or imagine" (Ephesians 3:20)? What changes might occur in our child's life as a result?

One thing is certain: Jesus *loves* that kind of faith.

And wouldn't you love to amaze Jesus?

The prince of darkness grim,
we tremble not for him.
His rage we can endure,
for lo' his doom is sure.
One little word shall fell him.

MARTIN LUTHER, "A MIGHTY FORTRESS IS OUR GOD"

For Chains to Fall

He brought them out of darkness and the deepest gloom
and broke away their chains.

PSALM 107:14

You've broken so many chains, Lord!
You did it for Joseph in prison (Genesis 41:14).
You did when you set your people free from Pharaoh (Exodus 12:51).
You did if for Daniel (Daniel 6:23)
    and Shadrach and Meshach and Abednego (Daniel 3:26).
You brought your people out of Babylon (Ezra 2:1).
You even sent an angel to Peter in prison,
    "and the chains fell off Peter's wrists" (Acts 12:7).
My son has his chains too, Lord.
They're not made of iron. They're made from sins he forged of his own
    free will, thinking they would bring him more freedom.
They've done anything but that.
    They've only kept him from coming closer to you.
You promised that "if the Son sets you free,
    you will be free indeed" (John 8:36).
Your Word says, "The LORD sets prisoners free" (Psalm 146:7).
Set him free, Lord! He needs you to break his chains.
I ask to hear the sound of chains falling with a dull thud,
    never to be put on again.
I long to hear my son say, "The LORD has done great things" for me,
    and I am "filled with joy" (Psalm 126:3).
I long for him to say to you, "I run in the path of your commands,
    for you have set my heart free" (Psalm 119:32).
Please give him grace to understand that obedience to you is the best
    kind of freedom, because it enables him to be the person you
    created him to be.

Help him to see that when he is conformed "to the pattern of this
world" (Romans 12:2), it is the worst kind of slavery:
"bondage to decay" (Romans 8:21).
Father, I know only part of the challenges he's facing, but you know
all of them.
I ask that you will break his chains link by link, so that he will turn
to you.
I pray that the things that once captivated him will lose their lure,
and he will understand they are "the devil's trap" (1 Timothy 3:7).
I pray he will come to his "senses and escape from the trap of the
devil, who has taken" him "captive to do his will"
(2 Timothy 2:26).
You've set so many free, Father! I ask that you do the same for my son.
Let him say of you, "My heart trusts in him, and I am helped.
My heart leaps for joy" (Psalm 28:7).
Let him leap, Lord! A leap of faith out of his chains and straight
to you.

For an Honest Answer

An honest answer is like a kiss on the lips.

PROVERBS 24:26

I remember honest answers, Lord.

When my son was little, he'd say things so truthfully.

I loved those moments! The innocent questions an adult would never
ask, the 'just the facts' statements that left no room for doubt.

I pray for honesty for my son, Father. He's been struggling with that
recently.

Help him to work hard to keep his
"conscience clear before God and man" (Acts 24:16).

I ask that you will help him to understand the damage that dishonesty
does to his relationships with others.

Help him to grasp the fact that "the man of integrity walks securely,
but he who takes crooked paths will be found out"
(Proverbs 10:9).

Father, please give him grace to *want* to be a man of integrity
who can look others in the eye and "speak the truth"
(Zechariah 8:16).

Help me to be honest with him and to resist the temptation to
compromise the truth in any way, simply because he hasn't been
honest with me.

I ask that he will understand that in order to be trusted,
he has to be trustworthy.

He wants me to trust him. I pray that you will help him see the
disconnect between what he wants and his actions.

Help him to become "blameless and pure," a child of God "without
fault in a crooked and depraved generation" (Philippians 2:15).

Touch his heart, Lord, so he can understand what you meant when
you said that "whoever can be trusted with very little can also be
trusted with much" (Luke 16:10).

Help him to be honest in the little things as well as the larger ones.

I know he lies to me sometimes because he knows
   that I'll disapprove of something he's done.
Father, please help him understand that though he may hide from me,
   he can never hide from you.
"You are the God who sees" (Genesis 16:13).
You "desire truth in the inner parts" (Psalm 51:6).
You told us that we must give an account
   for every "careless word" we have spoken (Matthew 12:36).
"I know, my God, that you test the heart and are pleased with
   integrity" (1 Chronicles 29:17).
I pray that he will walk in the truth (3 John 1:3),
   and that the truth will live in him (2 John 3).
You are the truth, Lord (John 14:6), and "your word is truth"
   (John 17:17).
I pray that he will "know the truth," and the truth will set him free
   (John 8:32) to live in your joy forever.

Off Broadway

Enter through the narrow gate. For wide is the gate and broad is the road that leads to destruction, and many enter through it. But small is the gate and narrow the road that leads to life, and only a few find it.

MATTHEW 7:13–14

She's seen enough, Lord.
Enough entertainment to negatively impact her outlook on life
    and lead her astray from what is really living.
I pray you will loosen the grip of media on her heart and mind,
    Father.
Help her to be mindful of the movies she watches and the music she
    listens to.
Instead of the lyrics of popular songs filling her head,
    I pray that you will help her to hide your Word in her heart,
    that she "might not sin against you" (Psalm 119:11).
I ask that you open her eyes to the emptiness of the ways of this
    world.
Give her wisdom to see that those who live for this world
    are living for "what does not satisfy" (Isaiah 55:2).
Let her see the shallowness of it.
    Lift her out of self-focus and let her look to you.
Help her understand not only how those who seem to 'have
    everything' live, but also how they *die*: unhappy, unfulfilled, and
    separated from you.
Bring her to the place where she can genuinely ask, "What good is it
    for a man to gain the whole world, yet forfeit his soul?"
    (Mark 8:36).
The world around her idolizes actors and actresses and models
    and singers.
Please help her see the difference between fame and true success.
Lord Jesus, let her look to you as the example for her life.

"Whoever follows" you "will never walk in darkness,
but will have the light of life" (John 8:12).
Direct her feet from the broad way "that leads to destruction" and on
to the narrow road "that leads to life" that "only a few find."
Let her life reflect your goodness, so that she is transformed into your
"likeness with ever-increasing glory" (2 Corinthians 3:18).
"Whatever is right, whatever is pure, whatever is lovely, whatever is
admirable," help her to "think about such things."
Then you, "the God of peace," will be with her (Philippians 4:8–9).
I pray that she will come to understand that the real purpose of life
is not to be entertained, but to "walk with" you (Revelation 3:4).
I pray that "your name and renown" will become "the desire of our
hearts," hers and mine, today and always (Isaiah 26:8)!

Taming the Tongue

*All kinds of animals, birds, reptiles and creatures of the sea
are being tamed and have been tamed by man, but no man can
tame the tongue. It is a restless evil, full of deadly poison.*

JAMES 3:7–8

Profanity is everywhere he turns, Lord—
    at school, at work, in so many forms of entertainment—
    and because the world finds it acceptable,
    he's been tempted to think the same way.
I pray that you would help him understand that what comes out of his
    mouth is more than 'just words.'
"Out of the overflow of the heart the mouth speaks" (Matthew 12:34).
Help him to see that swearing doesn't make him tough or more of a
    man, it makes him less of one.
It dishonors you and demonstrates a lack of character and self-control.
It parrots the world and shows a want of creativity.
Help him to be more careful with his words, Lord.
You've told us "that men will have to give account on the day
    of judgment for every careless word they have spoken"
    (Matthew 12:36).
I ask that you will make his conscience sensitive to every foul
    or inappropriate word that he hears.
Let him be repulsed by it, so that he loses the attraction to music or
    movies or friends that assault his ears.
Help him not to make compromises with the world. Give him grace to
    "avoid every kind of evil" (1 Thessalonians 5:22).
Remind him that "the good man brings good things out of the good
    stored up in him, and the evil man brings evil things out of the
    evil stored up in him" (Matthew 12:35).
I pray he will take a stand in his own heart and mind and "fight the
    good fight, holding on to faith and a good conscience" (1 Timothy
    1:18–19).

He can't do it on his own, Father.

Your Word says that "no man can tame the tongue."

But you can. You can fill him with your Spirit,
if he will only let you. I pray that he will!

Then he will be able to "get rid of all moral filth and the evil that is so
prevalent and humbly accept the word planted" in him, "which
can save" him (James 1:21).

Then he will be "controlled not by the sinful nature but by the Spirit,"
because "the Spirit of God lives in" him (Romans 8:9).

I pray that instead of a torrent of foul words, "streams of living water
will flow from within him" (John 7:38), because he believes
in you!

Run!

*Flee from sexual immorality . . . Do you not know that your body
is a temple of the Holy Spirit, who is in you, whom you have
received from God? You are not your own; you were bought
at a price. Therefore honor God with your body.*

1 Corinthians 6:18–20

It's all around him, Lord.
On the Internet, on TV, in magazines, and in the people he meets
    every day.
Sexual immorality reaches its poison claw out to him at every turn.
Your Word tells us that we can take our
    "stand against the devil's schemes" (Ephesians 6:11).
But when it comes to sexual immorality, you tell us to "flee"!
Father, please give him grace to see the danger and run!
Help him understand that sexual immorality threatens the health of
    his body and wages "war against" his soul (1 Peter 2:11).
Help him to "put to death . . . whatever belongs" to his "earthly nature:
    sexual immorality, impurity, lust, evil desires and greed,
    which is idolatry."
Give him grace to understand that "because of these,
    the wrath of God is coming" (Colossians 3:5–6),
    and you "will punish men for all such sins" (1 Thessalonians 4:6).
I pray that he will turn to you "with reverence and awe" (Hebrews 12:28),
    "so that the fear of God will be with" him
    to keep him "from sinning" (Exodus 20:20).
I pray that he will "learn to control his own body in a way that is holy
    and honorable" (1 Thessalonians 4:4).
Help him to turn his head, knowing "that anyone who looks at a
    woman lustfully has already committed adultery with her in his
    heart" (Matthew 5:28).
When temptation says, "Come to bed with me!" (Genesis 39:12),
    let him run and not look back.

Teach him the priceless value of innocence and purity, Father.
Help him take to heart that "the sexually immoral"
    "will not inherit the kingdom of God" (1 Corinthians 6:9).
I pray he will understand that lust is not love,
    and that love is a gift of your creating.
Because you invented love, I pray he will honor you with it.
Whatever mistakes he's made, please give him grace to see
    that your kindness leads him "toward repentance" (Romans 2:4).
He can make a fresh start with you!
Cleanse his temple and fill him with your Holy Spirit
    (1 Corinthians 6:19).
Let there be no doubt that he belongs to you, body and soul,
    because you "bought" him "at a price" (1 Corinthians 6:20).
May the price of your body, given for him,
    give him every inspiration to give his own to you.

For Freedom from Substance Abuse

*Be careful, or your hearts will be weighed down with dissipation,
drunkenness and the anxieties of life.*

LUKE 21:34

He's not being careful, Lord.
His heart is "weighed down with dissipation, drunkenness
and the anxieties of life," and he doesn't even know it.
He's given in to the world's message that he's 'having a good time,'
but he isn't.
He's complicated his life in ways that hurt to see.
"Who has woe? Who has sorrow? Who has strife? Who has complaints?
Who has needless bruises? Who has bloodshot eyes?
Those who linger over wine" (Proverbs 23:29–30).
There's been too much lingering, Lord. He likes it too much.
And "in the end it bites like a snake and poisons like a viper"
(Proverbs 23:32).
But I praise you, Father. You are the one who says "to the captives,
'Come out,' and to those in darkness, 'Be free!'" (Isaiah 49:9).
Call him out, Lord! Out of darkness, out of dissipation, out of any
substance or drug abuse, and out of relationships that contribute
to these things.
I can see him set free, Lord. Shining from head to foot, smiling and
strong, a living example of your kindness and love.
He has "spent enough time in the past
doing what pagans choose to do" (1 Peter 4:3).
Set him free, Father!
I know that he has to *want* to be free. So I ask you to open his eyes
to see the consequences of his actions, and let him long for
something more.
Let him "hunger and thirst for righteousness,"
for then he "will be filled" and blessed (Matthew 5:6)!

Let him "be filled with the Spirit" (Ephesians 5:18),
   because "where the Spirit of the Lord is,
   there is freedom" (2 Corinthians 3:17).
Lord Jesus, you came "to proclaim freedom for the captives and
   release from darkness for the prisoners" (Isaiah 61:1).
Help my son, Lord—he's a prisoner of his addictions.
I pray that he be "brought into the glorious freedom of the children of
   God" in every way (Romans 8:21)!
I thank you that you are completely able to do this, Father.
You are able to keep him "from falling and to present" him before your
   "glorious presence without fault and with great joy" (Jude 1:24).
Let your joy be so real to him that he won't seek happiness in
   anything less.
I praise you in advance for the day he will tell you,
   "You have filled my heart with greater joy" (Psalm 4:7).
O Father, let that day be today!

Praise for Small Victories

Who despises the day of small things?

ZECHARIAH 4:10

Thank you, Father. There's progress in my daughter's life right now.
No one else may see it, but it's definitely there.
It is the work of your hand.
I praise you that this is only the beginning.
You will continue to move, and you will continue to answer prayer,
    because if we ask anything according to your will, you hear us
    (1 John 5:14).
You do not want "anyone to perish, but everyone to come
            to repentance" (2 Peter 3:9).
You want my daughter to come to you even more than I do,
    and you are drawing her to yourself.
I praise you for this "day of small things," Father (Zechariah 4:10),
    and I thank you it will turn into something much greater.
I look forward to the day my daughter will be all she can be, through
    your "incomparably great power for us who believe"
    (Ephesians 1:19).
That is the same power you used to raise Jesus from the dead,
    and to make me alive in Him when I was
    "dead in transgressions" (Ephesians 2:5).
If you can do it for me, you can do it for her as well!
Thank you that you are already at work.
I can *see* that now, Father, and I praise you for this small step forward
    in my daughter's life, the first of many more steps to come.
"Faith is being sure of what we hope for
    and certain of what we do not see" (Hebrews 11:1).
Through faith I see her coming ever closer to you—forgiven,
    saved, restored, set free.
I see you using the mistakes she has made to call others "out of the
    darkness" and into your "wonderful light" (1 Peter 2:9).

I praise you for today's victory and mark it with Samuel's words:
"Thus far has the LORD helped us" (1 Samuel 7:12)!
Thank you for the days to come, in which you will help her
even more!
My "Redeemer is strong; the LORD Almighty is his name"
(Jeremiah 50:34)!
Keep moving, Lord! Thank you for hearing my prayers!
I am confident that you will carry "on to completion" the "good work"
you have begun in her (Philippians 1:6).
Please give me grace to "fight the good fight" of faith
until that day comes (1 Timothy 1:18)!

Coming to Our Senses

When he came to his senses, he said, "How many of my father's hired men have food to spare, and here I am starving to death!"

LUKE 15:17

Esther was worried about her son. Edwin was only three years old, the youngest of five children, and he was very sick.

The local doctor wasn't sure of the illness but he was worried as well. He suspected leukemia. When Edwin was taken to the hospital for further testing, the results confirmed the doctor's worst fear: an aggressive form of leukemia.

It was the middle of the Great Depression and effective treatment of the disease was decades away. Blood transfusions were prescribed and Edwin's father, Jasper, was a match.

Jasper gave heroically, providing as much blood as doctors would allow. But Edwin continued to decline. Jasper and Esther hung on to hope and prayed ardently. Esther stayed close to Edwin through the night, watching and praying and caring for her little son as best she could.

Late one night, when the room was quiet, Esther heard the distinct sound of singing. She couldn't make out the words, but she later described it as the most beautiful music she had ever heard. It soothed her soul and wiped the worry from her brow. Like Jacob at Bethel, she found herself standing at "the gate of heaven" (Genesis 28:17), in the very presence of God.

The next morning she told Jasper, "Whatever happens, everything is going to be all right. I just know it. Last night, I heard angels singing."

Edwin died that day. Jasper, weakened by the frequent transfusions, contracted pneumonia and died a few months later at the age of thirty-nine. Esther was pregnant, and the son she was carrying would never know his father.

Esther never remarried, but it wasn't for lack of opportunity. She was a beautiful young woman with sparkling blue eyes.

She never became bitter. She kept her faith and the God of her faith kept her, and cared for her every need to the end of her days. By the time I met her, her hair was white, but her eyes were still a sparkling blue. She talked to me about Jesus and made the best homemade doughnuts this side of heaven.

Esther was my maternal grandmother.

There is a strength God gives His own that is unmistakable. It cannot be rationalized or understood apart from His presence. As Pascal wrote, "the heart has its reasons, which reason does not know."[1] Sometimes *you know* that God will show himself faithful, come what may. Through faithful prayer and the touch of His Spirit, God gives the gift of "the peace of God, which transcends all understanding," that guards our hearts and our "minds in Christ Jesus" (Philippians 4:7).

That's why prayer is "the Christian's vital breath." God uses it to give us grace that we would never encounter otherwise. For the parents of prodigals, prayer is a lifeline. Just as my grandmother found supernatural strength through prayer when her son was physically dying, God will use it to impart power to parents when the souls of their children are in need of salvation.

That lifeline moves through us to our children. God uses our prayers to reach our children wherever they may be, and to accomplish good in their lives that would not have occurred if we were not praying. Regardless of the distance, "the arm of the LORD is not too short to save, nor his ear too dull to hear" (Isaiah 59:1). The prodigal son "came to his senses" in a far country (Luke 15:17).

The parents of prodigals may "come to their senses" as well, especially where prayer is concerned. God frequently moves through our challenging circumstances to cause us to pray more than we ever have before. He uses our prayers to pull us close and show us what He alone can do. He sharpens our "spiritual senses," giving us

---

1. Pascal, *Pensees*, section IV, number 277, available at http://www.ccel.org/ccel/pascal/pensees.v.html.

the peace that we so desperately need and a fresh strength that we never knew was possible.

We may even hear angels sing.

Jesus said "there is rejoicing in the presence of the angels of God over one sinner who repents" (Luke 15:10). And in His presence, there is all the help that we need.

Prayer is the Christian's vital breath,
the Christian's native air.
His watchword at the gates of death;
he enters heav'n with prayer.

JAMES MONTGOMERY, "PRAYER IS THE SOUL'S SINCERE DESIRE"

When You've Said Something You Regret

Set a guard over my mouth, O Lord;
keep watch over the door of my lips.

PSALM 141:3

I did it again, Lord. I spoke to my child in anger,
  and it wasn't the right response.
I know there are times when I'm permitted to be angry at the wrong
  in her life, but your Word also says, "In your anger do not sin"
  (Psalm 4:4).
I went too far and said things I should not have said.
Forgive me, Lord, and give me fresh grace.
Because you give "grace to the humble" (Proverbs 3:34),
  I humble myself before you and ask you to show me
  "the most excellent way" (1 Corinthians 12:31).
I know that "if I speak in the tongues of men and of angels, but have
  not love, I am only a resounding gong or a clanging cymbal"
  (1 Corinthians 13:1).
I also know that "man's anger does not bring about the righteous life
  that God desires" (James 1:20).
So I ask you to help me to do the hard thing and ask for my child's
  forgiveness.
I pray that you will give her grace to accept my apology
  so that our relationship can be healed.
I really want to "do everything in love," Father (1 Corinthians 16:14),
  but right now I find parenting so difficult.
I need you to take up "my case" and "uphold my cause" (Lamentations
  3:58–59) so that she will see you at work even in this situation.
You are the one "who daily bears our burdens" (Psalm 68:19),
  and I ask you to carry me through this and give me wisdom.
I thank you that you can take even actions with imperfect motives
  and use them "for good" and "the saving of many lives"
  (Genesis 50:20).

"Set a guard over my mouth, O Lord" (Psalm 141:3)
  so that "the fruit of righteous will be peace" (Isaiah 32:17).
May the word of Christ dwell in me richly so that I may "teach and
  admonish" "with all wisdom" (Colossians 3:16).
You, "speaking in righteousness," are "mighty to save" (Isaiah 63:1).
Whisper your truth to my daughter's heart, Lord, and save her!
You are "able to save completely" those who come to you
  (Hebrews 7:25).
Let her come to you, Lord!
You said, "I have loved you with an everlasting love;
  I have drawn you with loving-kindness" (Jeremiah 31:3).
Draw her with love, Father!
I love you because you loved me first (1 John 4:19).
Please do the same for my child.
"May the words of my mouth and the meditation of my heart be
  pleasing in your sight" (Psalm 19:14) so that her "joy in Christ
  Jesus will overflow on account of me" (Philippians 1:26).

Manipulated

You intended to harm me, but God intended it for good to accomplish
what is now being done, the saving of many lives.

GENESIS 50:20

Here we go again, Lord.
I've been manipulated once again.
I want to believe the best things about my child,
    but sometimes he takes advantage of that!
He wants me to trust him, and I want to be able to!
And then something happens that makes trust difficult.
But it's not just my son who is doing the manipulating, Father.
He's being manipulated by the Adversary and he doesn't even know it.
He's being conformed to "the pattern of this world," when he needs to
    be transformed by the renewing of his mind (Romans 12:2).
He's being deceived (Genesis 3:13), and my heart aches for him.
But this battle for his heart and his mind is not over.
"The battle is the LORD's" (1 Samuel 17:47).
"To him belong strength and victory;
    both deceived and deceiver are his" (Job 12:16).
I have already given my son to you, Father, and I give him to
    you again.
Just like you prayed for Peter, Lord Jesus, when the devil went after
    him, I pray that my son's "faith may not fail" (Luke 22:31–32).
"Spirit of truth," I ask that you guide him "into all truth" (John 16:13)
    so that he will "overcome the evil one" (1 John 2:13).
Father, although my son has been deceived, I pray that you will use
    even this circumstance "for good" and "the saving of many lives"!
When he turns, let him turn others to you.
Then "no weapon forged against" us will prevail (Isaiah 54:17).
I look forward to the day when I will be able to look my son in the eye
    and know that he is telling the truth,
        because he is "walking in the truth" (2 John 1:4).

What a joy that will be!

I praise you in advance for the day my son's faith will be restored,
    when he will shout to you with gratitude,
    "You have become my salvation" (Psalm 118:21)!

"Hallelujah! Salvation and glory and power belong to our God"
    (Revelation 19:1)!

The victory will be yours, and the blessing will be ours!

Amen.

Songs in the Night

*By day the L*ORD *directs his love, at night his song is with me—*
a prayer to the God of my life.

PSALM 42:8

I can't sleep, Lord, and you know why.
I'm worried about my child.
I know you told me not to worry about *my* life (Matthew 6:25),
    but is it OK if I talk to you about hers?
I remember when she was just a baby, and things were so much easier.
Thank you for those days. They were a gift!
But you know the situation we're in now, Father.
I never saw this coming. Not like this.
    Do any parents think their child will go through prodigal years?
I always thought things like this happen to *other* people,
    and I have to admit I've sometimes been too quick
    to come up with a reason *why.*
It's easier to parent someone else's kids in our own minds
    without knowing what those parents are really going through,
    isn't it?
My daughter and I are up against it tonight, Lord, and we need you
    so much.
I need the peace "which transcends all understanding"
    to guard my heart and mind in you (Philippians 4:7).
She needs your light to shine on her path and lead her
    "from darkness to light" (Acts 26:18).
You are "the light of the world," Lord Jesus (John 8:12).
    And you are my light tonight.
You are "God my Maker, who gives songs in the night" (Job 35:10).
I stand on the promise of your Word tonight:
    "Surely God is my salvation; I will trust and not be afraid.
    The LORD, the LORD, is my strength and my song;
    he has become my salvation" (Isaiah 12:2).

Thank you that when I "do not know what to do"
(2 Chronicles 20:12),
I can look to you for the direction I need.
You are "the way and the truth and the life" (John 14:6).
"With you is the fountain of life; in your light we see light"
(Psalm 36:9).
I place this situation in your hands, Lord, and cast on you
every worry, every need, every care (Psalm 55:22).
You said, "Come to me, all you who are weary and burdened,
and I will give you rest" (Matthew 11:28).
That describes me pretty well right now, so I come.
And I bring my child with me in the arms of faith and prayer.
I praise you because your "light shines in the darkness,"
and the darkness will not overcome it (John 1:5).
"I will lie down and sleep in peace" (Psalm 4:8),
because you are my hope.
The future looks bright with you!

Accepting Rejection   *1-15-16*

*He was despised and rejected by men, a man of sorrows,
and familiar with suffering. Like one from whom men hide
their faces he was despised, and we esteemed him not.*

ISAIAH 53:3

Father, right now my child doesn't understand that if I really love her,
　　I'm not going to let her do whatever she wants.
She's angry with me about that, and we need your help.
I pray that in her anger, she will not sin and choose to do
　　what I've told her she cannot.
I pray that the devil will not gain a foothold in this
　　(Ephesians 4:26–27).
I ask instead that your peace will rule in her heart (Colossians 3:15).
I also ask that you will protect her from friends
　　who would lead her "astray" (Proverbs 12:26).
Father, I pray that you would not allow the "bitter root" of defiance
　　to take hold in any way (Hebrews 12:15).
Instead, "let salvation spring up, let righteousness grow with it"
　　(Isaiah 45:8).
I pray that she will mature through this
　　and "reject the wrong and choose the right" (Isaiah 7:16).
I ask that you would quietly speak to her and teach her "your way,
　　O LORD" so that she will "walk in your truth"
　　with an "undivided heart" (Psalm 86:11).
Help her to understand not only how much I love her, but most of all,
　　how much you do.
You know what it's like to have those you love reject you,
　　because you came to earth and we "did not receive" you
　　(John 1:11).
You chose to accept our rejection for our own benefit, to save us and
　　set us free.
In a small way I'm beginning to understand some of that, Lord.

It's *because* I love her that I'm trying to help her to choose what is right, despite her defiance.

Thank you, Father, for doing that for us.

Your Word makes this so very clear:

Even when we were your "enemies," you chose to reconcile us "through the death" of your son (Romans 5:10).

"This is love: not that we loved God, but that he loved us and sent his Son as an atoning sacrifice for our sins" (1 John 4:10).

Dear Jesus, I commit my daughter to you afresh.

Rescue her from this world, Lord, and keep her from the mistake of choosing her way over your own.

Your Word says, "Whoever turns a sinner from the error of his way will save him from death and cover over a multitude of sins" (James 5:20).

Thank you for saving me. Save her too, I pray!

When Distance Separates

Surely the arm of the LORD is not too short to save,
nor his ear too dull to hear.

ISAIAH 59:1

Father, I thank you there is nowhere my son can go
    where you are not already present.
Even though he is far from me,
    I rest in the promise that your arm "is not too short to save."
I pray that you will meet him where he is, Lord.
Let him encounter you everywhere he turns, "behind and before"
    (Psalm 139:5).
Open his eyes to "paths of life" that lead in your direction
    and draw him close to you (Acts 2:28).
Father, he needs you to point him home.
Not home to me, but to his eternal home with you.
Just like the prodigal son who "came to his senses" in a far country,
    I ask that he will become aware of anything that separates him
    from you.
May he say, "I will set out and go back to my father"
    and run to your open arms (Luke 15:17–18).
Even where he is now, he is not so far away that your love cannot
    reach him, because "the earth is filled with your love, O LORD"
    (Psalm 119:64).
Let your love surround him and keep him from all harm.
Father, give him "more grace" to submit himself to you and
    "resist the devil," so the devil "will flee" from him (James 4:6–7).
Fill his heart with faith, because then he will be helped in every way
    and "shielded" by your power (1 Peter 1:5).
Send your angels to help him, as you do for those who "inherit
    salvation" (Hebrews 1:14).
I pray you will bring him new friends who know you,
    and keep him from those who would lead him astray.

Give him a longing to be part of "the family of believers" (Galatians 6:10), where he will be encouraged, helped, and blessed.

Let every road that he takes lead to you, Lord.

Thank you, Father, that you hear my prayer.

Thank you that you are even more willing to answer than I am to ask.

I praise you that you are "able to do immeasurably more than all we ask or imagine" (Ephesians 3:20).

I praise you for the ways you will answer this prayer!

Praise in the Dark /-/5-/६

About midnight Paul and Silas were praying and singing hymns
to God, and the other prisoners were listening to them.

Acts 16:25

What Paul and Silas did was beautiful and inspiring, Father.
Even though they had been "stripped" and "severely flogged" and
were in a dark jail cell after midnight with their feet in stocks,
they were praising you (Acts 16:22–24)!
What an amazing example! Please give me grace to do the same when
I feel defeated and in the dark.
I want to give you the glory due your name (1 Chronicles 16:29)
and continue praising you even when I don't know what the
next day brings.
You are always worthy of praise.
When I don't 'feel like' drawing near to you, that's when I need to
praise you most of all, because you "strengthen the feeble hands"
and "steady the knees that give way."
You "say to those with fearful hearts, 'Be strong, do not fear;
your God will come'" (Isaiah 35:3–4).
When it's the middle of the night and I'm wondering if my child
is safe, I will find "courage to pray to you" (1 Chronicles 17:25).
Just as David "found strength in the Lord his God" when his family
was in danger (1 Samuel 30:6), I know you can give me grace to
persevere.
"My heart says of you, 'Seek his face!'
Your face, Lord, I will seek" (Psalm 27:8).
I pray for grace to seek "your face with all my heart" (Psalm 119:58).
When I'm wondering why things have happened even though I have
been trying to parent my child as well as I can, I will "not rely on"
myself "but on" you (2 Corinthians 1:9).

When it feels like my prayers are bouncing off the ceiling and going
no farther,
I thank you that my faith is not dependent upon feelings.
I praise you, Lord Jesus, that even when our faith is weak
you "will remain faithful" (2 Timothy 2:13).
I've never been through anything like what happened to Paul
and Silas, but if you gave them strength to praise you then,
and you are "the same yesterday and today and forever"
(Hebrews 13:8), then you can do the same for me.
Together, we will win "the victory" in my child's life (1 John 5:4).
May she see your Spirit in me, and may it draw her to you.
Then we will praise you together, our Savior and our God!

Constant Help

God is our refuge and strength, an ever-present help in trouble.

Psalm 46:1

Father, you're not just an 'occasional help' when times are tough.
I praise you because you're an "ever-present help"!
There is never a day, an hour, a minute, or a moment when you are not
    attentive.
You are truly amazing, God! You "neither slumber nor sleep"
    (Psalm 121:4).
Nothing gets past you. Not a "careless word" (Matthew 12:36)
    or the inclination of our thoughts (Genesis 6:5).
Even the hairs of our heads "are all numbered" (Luke 12:7).
Because you give constant help, I trust in you (Psalm 115:11).
Because your name is a "strong tower,"
    I'm going to keep running to you (Proverbs 18:10). *1–15–16 Rn.*
You give me the strength to go on (Psalm 29:11).
You know why I'm here, Lord. I'm here to ask for your mercy and help.
I know that apart from you, I can do nothing (John 15:5).
I come to you for my child again, and I'm going to keep coming as
    long as you give me "breath" (Isaiah 42:5).
Isn't that what your Word says?
"You who call on the Lord, give yourselves no rest" (Isaiah 62:6–7).
You want me to keep coming to you for my child again and again.
You want me to "pray continually" (1 Thessalonians 5:17).
So I make this prayer my *declaration of dependence* on you.
You know how my child will return to you. You know the day
    and the hour. You know exactly what it will take.
Thank you, Father, that you never tire of hearing my prayers
    for my child.
Thank you, Lord Jesus, that you are able to save my son "completely,"
    and that you go to the Father for us every day (Hebrews 7:25).

Thank you, Holy Spirit, that when I don't know exactly what to pray,
you intercede for me "with groans that words cannot express"
(Romans 8:26).

I will "approach the throne of grace with confidence, so that we may
receive mercy and find grace to help us in our time of need"
(Hebrews 4:16).

I will come to you for him again and again, like the mother
who kept crying out to you for her daughter (Matthew 15:23),
and the father who begged you to look at his son (Luke 9:38).

Until my son runs to you, and you take him in your arms and bless
him, I will keep praying, day after day.

And then I'll pray again, thanking you with all my heart, "proclaiming
aloud your praise and telling of all your wonderful deeds"
(Psalm 26:7).

Treasured in Our Hearts

Then he went down to Nazareth with them and was obedient to them.
But his mother treasured all these things in her heart.

LUKE 2:51

When Jesus was a boy, Mary and Joseph left him behind in Jerusalem without knowing it. He was "in the temple courts" when they found him, "sitting among the teachers, listening to them and asking them questions" (Luke 2:46). Mary asked for an explanation, and Jesus answered, "Why were you searching for me? . . . Didn't you know I had to be in my Father's house?" (Luke 2:49).

She wasn't sure what he meant at the time. But she did know *something* was happening. Something beautiful. Something good. God was at work, and Mary understood that. So she "treasured all these things in her heart" (Luke 2:51).

I have some treasures too. Treasured memories from the Father's house when Katie was little. Bright eyes on sunny Sundays, taking it all in: "Look what I made you, Daddy!" A crayon card from Sunday school. Cuddling as close as she could when she sat beside me in worship. Simple prayers offered with a child's soaring faith. A little, lilting voice singing sweetly: "Jesus loves me, this I know . . ."

Jesus *loved* my little girl, and she *knew* it. Her childlike faith was simple and sincere, a gift from heaven untainted by the world. Like Mary, I could see that something was happening. God was at work in her little life. And that continues to give me hope.

Today's difficult days won't last forever. God is faithful. The seeds that grew and bloomed in the springtime of my daughter's life will one day flower again.

This is more than wishful thinking. The promises in God's Word give me hope. Promises like "From everlasting to everlasting the

LORD's love is with those who fear him, and his righteousness with their children's children" (Psalm 103:17), and "For the LORD is good and his love endures forever; his faithfulness continues through all generations" (Psalm 100:5).

I am resolved to pray for my daughter every day, and I take comfort in the fact that God looks forward to the day she returns to her faith even more than I.

G. K. Chesterton wrote that "we have sinned and grown old, and our Father is younger than we."[1] God abounds with life. Though He was "before all ages" (Jude 1:25), He knows no age. His strength is unfathomable: "The LORD is the everlasting God, the Creator of the ends of the earth. He will not grow tired or weary" (Isaiah 40:28). The seemingly limitless energy children have is just a pale reflection of His infinite, unfailing strength.

His amazing strength is able to pursue my daughter long after my own is gone. Because of His faithfulness, the prayers I've placed before the Father's throne will still be there, waiting to be answered in His perfect wisdom and way. E. M. Bounds, a minister and chaplain during the Civil War, understood this: "God shapes the world by prayer. Prayers are deathless. The lips that uttered them may be closed in death, the heart that felt them may have ceased to beat, but the prayers live before God, and God's heart is set on them. Prayers outlive the lives of those who uttered them; outlive a generation, outlive an age, outlive a world."[2]

"God's heart is set on them." He will receive the prayers offered in faith with an everlasting love that "never fails" (1 Corinthians 13:8).

So I will run to Him for her. I will pour out my heart in prayer, knowing that He is completely in agreement that she needs to turn her heart to Him. I will carry her to Him in the arms of prayer, because I still treasure her in my heart, and I always will.

As much as I treasure her, He treasures her more. If her childhood faith is precious to me, the worth of it to Him is incalculable.

So here she is, Father, our treasured child: yours, mine, ours.

I bring her to you once again.

---

1. Chesteron, *Orthodoxy*, 60.
2. Bounds, *Complete Works*, 299.

Your prayers, dear child of God . . . shall be answered—
some of them, perhaps, during your lifetime on earth,
and all of them, certainly, during your lifetime in heaven.

SAMUEL PRIME

When She Hasn't Come Home Yet

I am like a desert owl, like an owl among the ruins.
I lie awake; I have become like a bird alone on a roof.

PSALM 102:6–7

It's been one of those nights, Lord.
She should have been home hours ago.
So I sit here, waiting.
Waiting for the phone to ring.
Waiting for the sound of the car in the driveway
    and her footsteps on the front porch.
Be with her, Lord. You know where she is.
Please watch over her, Father, and keep her safe.
I thank you that you are still in control,
    regardless of the choices my child makes.
"How great you are, O Sovereign LORD!
There is no one like you, and there is no God but you"
    (2 Samuel 7:22).
"Even the darkness will not be dark to you; the night will shine
    like the day, for darkness is as light to you" (Psalm 139:12).
Even at this moment, turn her thoughts home.
Not just to me, but to you.
I want her to call home, but most of all I want her to call on
    your name.
"You are forgiving and good, O Lord,
    abounding in love to all who call to you" (Psalm 86:5).
"The LORD is near to all who call on him,
    to all who call on him in truth" (Psalm 145:18).
You richly bless all who call on you (Romans 10:12), because
    "everyone who calls on the name of the Lord will be saved"
    (Acts 2:21).
Please bring her home, Father. All the way home.

Let her heart be at home in your presence,
    because that's what she needs most of all.
I want her to obey me, Lord Jesus, but even more I want her
    to obey *you*.
You said, "If anyone loves me, he will obey my teaching.
    My Father will love him, and we will come to him
    and make our home with him" (John 14:23).
Your Word also says, "The children of your servants will live in
    your presence; their descendants will be established before you"
    (Psalm 102:28).
I'm holding on to that promise tighter than ever tonight, Lord,
    so please hold on to *her*, just as you said you would.
Take her by the hand.
Take her by the heart.
And lead her *home*.

Light His Feet

Your word is a lamp to my feet and a light for my path.

PSALM 119:105

Your Word is amazing, Father!
It has the power to transform lives.
It is "living and active. Sharper than any double-edged sword,
   it penetrates even to dividing soul and spirit, joints and marrow;
   it judges the thoughts and attitudes of the heart" (Hebrews 4:12–13).
How I love your Word!
I pray that you will release the power of your Word into my son's life.
Let your light fall on his feet and on his path.
So many people are telling him where to turn and what to do.
He needs to hear your voice, Lord.
"How can a young man keep his way pure?
   By living according to your word" (Psalm 119:9).
I pray that you will direct his "footsteps according to your word"
   and "let no sin rule over" him (Psalm 119:133).
Only you can lead him "in paths of righteousness"
   and restore his soul (Psalm 23:3).
He has a Bible. I pray that he will pick it up and read it!
Let him meet you in it, Father, and hear your voice in a way that he
   hasn't in a long time, because "you yourself" are teaching him
   (Psalm 119:102).
I pray you will open his eyes so that he "may see wonderful things"
   in your Word (Psalm 119:18).
Your Word is able to make him "wise for salvation through faith
   in Christ Jesus" (2 Timothy 3:15).
Bring his heart back to you as he reads so that there is no doubt
   about his relationship with you.
Give him a hunger for your Word—fill his heart and mind with it.
Let him turn to it every day, because "man does not live on bread
   alone, but on every word that comes from" you (Matthew 4:4).

As he spends time in your Word, let him see how you are speaking
to him about the intimate details of his life.

Then as a "man of God," "thoroughly equipped for every good work"
(2 Timothy 3:17), let him "speak your word with great boldness"
(Acts 4:29) so that others may hear it and love it too!

Shame Off Her!

As the Scripture says, "Anyone who trusts
in him will never be put to shame."

ROMANS 10:11

I can see my daughter standing before you, dressed in white.

It's her wedding day! But not on this earth.

There she is, in the kingdom of God, where your church is "prepared
as a bride beautifully dressed for her husband" (Revelation 21:2).

I pray that day will come for her, Lord Jesus!

That day in which she knows with all of her heart that whoever trusts
in you "will never be put to shame."

She trusted in you once, Lord, and I believe that you "began
a good work" in her and will "carry it on to completion"
(Philippians 1:6).

I pray you will move soon in her life to turn her heart from sin
back to you.

Let her hear your Spirit speaking to her: "I have swept away your
offenses like a cloud, your sins like the morning mist.
Return to me, for I have redeemed you" (Isaiah 44:22).

Let the fog clear and a bright new morning break!

Even when we rebel against you, you long for us to give our hearts
to you.

When we do, you take our sins completely away.

You clothe us with "garments of salvation"
and "a robe of righteousness" (Isaiah 61:10).

You present us holy in your sight,
"without blemish and free from accusation" (Colossians 1:22).

You have said, "You will forget the shame of your youth" (Isaiah 54:4).

And you choose to forget it as well!

You tell us you will remember our sins no more (Jeremiah 31:34).

Take the shame off my daughter, Lord Jesus! Just as you have for me.

You promise in your Word, "Do not be afraid; you will not suffer shame.
   Do not fear disgrace; you will not be humiliated" (Isaiah 54:4).
I pray my daughter will understand that when prodigals return,
   you throw a party!
You welcome them with arms held wide open!
Let her know deeply in her heart that there is no shame in being
   your child.
Let her know that any name she has been called doesn't matter,
   because one day, you will give a "new name" to all you have saved
   (Revelation 3:12), all who live for your kingdom and your love.
May any sin or shame from the past be washed away
   by your "precious blood" (1 Peter 1:19).
May she live so in love with you that others are drawn to you as well!
I know she has a choice to make, and I pray she will make it soon and
   "choose life" (Deuteronomy 30:19)!
I pray she will choose you!

What the Locusts Have Eaten

I will repay you for the years the locusts have eaten.

JOEL 2:25

"I will repay you for the years the locusts have eaten."
I love that promise, Lord. It shows me the kindness of your heart.
I praise you that there is no hurt that you cannot heal, no loss you
cannot restore.
You make "everything new" (Revelation 21:5)!
I look forward to the day you will make everything new in my
child's life.
You have a bright future waiting for her!
I pray she will open her heart to you and receive your mercy.
I thank you that even "the years the locusts have eaten"
can be turned to blessing, and I ask you to do that!
You are so resourceful, Father.
There is not a step my child has taken that cannot be one day turned
toward you.
You came to "those living in darkness and in the shadow of death,
to guide our feet into the path of peace" (Luke 1:79)
You tell the story, Jesus, of leaving ninety-nine sheep
to go after the one that is lost.
How wonderful you are to go after "lost sheep"!
When you find the lost one, you "rejoice" (Luke 15:4–6).
I ask that the damage the adversary has tried to cause in my child's life
will be completely undone so that *she will praise you*,
just as you long for her to do.
Your Word says, "from the lips of children and infants you have
ordained praise . . . to silence the foe and the avenger"
(Psalm 8:2).
I praise you too, Father.
I praise you because you love her with infinite love.
I long for my child to come home to you.

You long for that too, even more than I do, because you are "not
wanting anyone to perish, but everyone to come to repentance"
(2 Peter 3:9).

May she come to you *today*, Lord!

Let her heart be touched by your kindness
and her mind opened to the wonder of who you are.

Let her hear you say, "I am with you and will rescue you"
(Jeremiah 1:8).

Let her answer when you call and come running with a repenting
heart, drawn by the hope you alone can give.

You have said, "those who hope in me will not be disappointed"
(Isaiah 49:23). And she won't be!

You are my hope, Lord, and I pray that you soon will be hers.

"You are God my Savior, and my hope is in you all day long"
(Psalm 25:5).

Even though she doesn't know it now, I thank you that she will
one day "know the hope" to which you have called her
(Ephesians 1:18), and praise you for it with all of her heart.

Straight Steps

Trust in the LORD with all your heart and lean not on your own understanding; in all your ways acknowledge him, and he will make your paths straight.

PROVERBS 3:5–6

Sometimes I don't understand the choices my child makes, Lord.
He doesn't seem able to see the consequences of some actions
    and the pointlessness of others. Or he doesn't care.
He needs a breakthrough, Father. I ask that you lead him to one.
You are the "One who breaks open the way" (Micah 2:13)!
You promise in your Word, "I guide you in the way of wisdom
    and lead you along straight paths" (Proverbs 4:11).
I pray that promise for him today.
More than anything else, he needs to acknowledge you and trust you,
    because "the fear of the LORD is the beginning of wisdom"
    (Psalm 111:10).
I ask that you help him to think about eternity.
Help him to see that there is so much more to life
    than simply living for the moment.
Let him understand that the road he's on doesn't lead him to
    where he wants to be.
"Wide is the gate and broad is the road that leads to destruction,
    and many enter through it" (Matthew 7:13).
Let him turn from that road, Father!
I ask that you will give him grace to be "a wise son,
    endowed with intelligence and discernment" (2 Chronicles 2:12).
Make him "an upright man," who "gives thought to his ways"
    (Proverbs 21:29).
Place wise people in his path that he will listen to.
I ask that you will enable me to communicate with him so that he will
    listen, and that you will speak to him through me.
Your Word tells us to "get wisdom, get understanding" (Proverbs 4:5).

It also says, "Blessed is the man who finds wisdom . . . for she [wisdom] is more profitable than silver and yields better returns than gold" (Proverbs 3:13–14).

I want good things for my son, Father.

But most of all, I want what you can give him.

Your Word says that "to the man who pleases him, God gives wisdom, knowledge and happiness" (Ecclesiastes 2:26).

You are all of these things, Father, and so much more!

I ask that you make his steps straight so that they lead him straight to you!

Of God's Choosing

When I came to the spring today, I said, "O LORD,
God of my master Abraham, if you will, please grant
success to the journey on which I have come."

GENESIS 24:42

The way you answered Abraham's servant's prayer
for a wife for Isaac is beautiful, Father.
He was looking for your direction and blessing, and you gave it
to him.
I'd like to ask the same thing for my child, Lord.
You know exactly the right person to make the ideal spouse for her—
not just for earthly reasons, but for heavenly ones.
I ask for someone of your choosing.
I pray that you will lead my daughter to a man
who will be a blessing to her soul.
Wherever he is right now,
I ask that you bless him and prepare them both for one another.
I pray that he will be part of your purpose in calling her to yourself,
a man who loves you and "is known by" you (1 Corinthians 8:3).
I ask that even now you will move in his heart and mind to equip him
"with everything good" for doing your will, and that you would
work in him "what is pleasing" to you (Hebrews 13:21).
Let her see you at work in him and be drawn to you all the more
because of it.
Lord Jesus, let him love my daughter with a sacrificial love
that you alone can give, just as you loved the church
and gave yourself up for her (Ephesians 5:25).
I pray that love will be much more than simply a feeling for both
of them.
I ask that your "perfect love" (1 John 4:18) will be at work in them
so that they will both honor you above themselves,
and their marriage will stand the test of time.

I pray that he will "enjoy life" with the wife he loves (Ecclesiastes 9:9), and that your peace will rest upon the home they make together.

Bring them to the place where they can say together with all of their hearts, "As for me and my household, we will serve the LORD" (Joshua 24:15).

Let him "rejoice in the wife of" his youth (Proverbs 5:18), and let her be a source of blessing and joy to him.

Let them worship you "with gladness" (Psalm 100:2) for the gift of each other, and "praise you in the presence of your saints" (Psalm 52:9).

Father, I'd also like to ask you that you bless them with children who will walk with you so that "from generation to generation we will recount your praise" (Psalm 79:13).

I praise you in this moment for your kindness and faithfulness to answer this prayer, not only today, but in the years to come!

Inexhaustible

*Even youths grow tired and weary, and young men stumble
and fall; but those who hope in the LORD will renew their
strength. They will soar on wings like eagles; they will
run and not grow weary, they will walk and not be faint.*

ISAIAH 40:30–31

Someday she'll get tired, Lord.
Tired of this world and its false promises.
Tired of running from you.
On that day I pray that she will discover the strength that only you
can give.
Right now her energy seems boundless. But it won't last forever.
"Even youths grow tired and weary, and young men stumble and fall."
If she must stumble, I pray it will be into your arms.
If she must fall, I pray it will be in love with you.
Then she will find strength that she never knew was possible!
I praise you for the strength you give, Father.
You give "strength to the weary,"
and increase "the power of the weak" (Isaiah 40:29).
With you dwelling inside of her heart, she will have a source of energy
brighter than the sun, unlimited, infinite, eternal!
That's what you are, Father! Nothing compares to you!
I pray that she will find in you her "treasure in heaven that will not
be exhausted, where no thief comes near and no moth destroys"
(Luke 12:33).
Then, even when her body ages and her strength fails, she will not
"lose heart."
"Though outwardly we are wasting away, yet inwardly we are being
renewed day by day" by your inexhaustible mercy and love
(2 Corinthians 4:16).
I pray that she will run to you "and not grow weary."
I pray she will not only run, but soar!

Let her heart and mind take flight with the wonder of all that you are.
Let her humble herself under your "mighty hand,"
    that you may lift her up (1 Peter 5:6)!
Lifted in your hands, she *will* rise!
I pray she can "be strong and courageous," because you go with her,
    and you "will never leave" her "nor forsake" her (Deuteronomy 31:6).
Then she will hear you say, "You who dwell in the dust,
    wake up and shout for joy" (Isaiah 26:19)!
Then together we *will* shout for joy!
And we will sing your praise for all eternity!

Waiting for an Answer

But he did not answer her at all. And his disciples came and urged him,
saying, "Send her away, for she keeps shouting after us."

MATTHEW 15:23

When our daughter was fifteen she ran away.

Katie had fallen in with the wrong crowd at school. When we grounded her and pulled her out of school to finish the final weeks of her sophomore year at home, she made other plans. One day she ran out the door and down the street, where a friend picked her up in a car.

She was gone more than three weeks.

Those were the longest three weeks of our lives. Cari and I looked everywhere for our daughter and sought help from law enforcement and friends. But no matter how hard we tried, it seemed like we were always a few steps behind her.

Her life was in danger, and she didn't even know it. One day, Cari and I found ourselves sitting in the apartment of an armed drug dealer who knew some of Katie's friends and had seen her recently. Later, we discovered she was even a passenger in a wreck where the car rolled and others were injured. She left the scene when the police arrived.

In the desperate days that followed, Cari and I learned the importance of waiting on God in prayer for those we love.[1] We had no other choice. We had come to the end of our strength and resources and *had* to rely on God. The more we prayed, the more effective our search became.

---

1. Additional details of this lesson learned about prayer are shared in the author's book *The Lost Art of Praying Together*, chapter 6.

It was on a Father's Day that we found her. Cari and I were in a restaurant parking lot, on our way to dinner, when the phone rang. A waitress at another restaurant had spotted her. Katie was only three blocks away. We soon had her home, safe and sound.

God always answers prayer. The answer is either *yes*, *no*, or *wait*. When the answer is *wait*, it's easy to confuse it with no answer at all.

One of the more challenging stories from the Bible is Jesus' encounter with a Canaanite woman who "came to him, crying out, 'Lord, Son of David, have mercy on me! My daughter is suffering terribly from demon-possession.'"

The challenging part comes in the next verse: "Jesus did not answer a word" (Matthew 15:22–23).

Why? Didn't Jesus care about the woman and her daughter? Hadn't He come to "destroy the devil's work" (1 John 3:8)? What was Jesus doing?

Jesus' silence speaks volumes. We *have to wait* on God when we pray. We may not know how He will answer, but we do know He is pleased when we pursue Him and put our hearts before Him constantly in prayer.

The Canaanite woman persisted with Jesus. When he told her, "I was sent only to the lost sheep of Israel," she "came and knelt before him" and asked again. When He responded, "It is not right to take the children's bread and toss it to their dogs," that still didn't stop her.

"'Yes, Lord,' she said, 'but even the dogs eat the crumbs that fall from their masters' table.'"

Then came the answer she was longing to hear: "Woman, you have great faith! Your request is granted" (Matthew 15:24–28).

It took some time to get there. But she persisted because she loved her daughter and knew she was asking for something good for her.

The same is true when we pray for our prodigal kids. Sometimes the answers don't come when we would hope. Things may even seem to go from bad to worse. But we have to persevere, keep believing, and keep asking.

Like the Canaanite woman, we know we are asking for a good thing when we pray for God to change our children's hearts. We have the assurance that Jesus loves our children, because He died to make their salvation possible. When we ask Him to save them, we know we're praying for the very thing He wants to do.

Waiting is never easy, but the end result is worth it. David put it this way: "Those who know your name will trust in you, for you, LORD, have never forsaken those who seek you" (Psalm 9:10).

Keep seeking! Keep trusting! Keep asking! Keep praying!

There is grace to be found in the waiting, even if it takes years for the answer to come.

God's silence is never "the final word."

We must wait for God, long, meekly, in the wind and wet,
in the thunder and lightning, in the cold and the dark. Wait,
and he will come. He never comes to those who do not wait.

FREDERICK W. FABER

A Discerning Heart

Those who are wise will shine like the brightness of the heavens, and those who lead many to righteousness, like the stars for ever and ever.

DANIEL 12:3

Father, I love what Solomon asked of you when he was a very
    young man: "Give your servant a discerning heart . . . to
    distinguish between right and wrong" (1 Kings 3:9).
My son needs to distinguish between right and wrong, Father,
    and I also am in need of wisdom as I try to help him.
I pray that you will give a discerning heart to both of us.
I ask for your wisdom to parent this child, Father,
    and to discover all the right ways to point him to you.
My wisdom is so limited, Father. I can't do this without your help.
And I thank you that I have it!
I thank you for your promise that "if any of you lacks wisdom,
    he should ask God, who gives generously to all
    without finding fault" (James 1:5).
I praise you because you don't find fault, Father!
I ask for the discernment you alone can give, because "the wisdom of
    the world is foolishness" in your sight (1 Corinthians 3:19).
I pray that you will give us both "the wisdom that comes from
    heaven" that is "first of all pure" (James 3:17).
Help my son to understand that
    "knowledge of the Holy One is understanding" (Proverbs 9:10).
If he knows you, he has all that he needs!
Give him grace to know that "all the treasures of wisdom and
    knowledge" are hidden in Christ (Colossians 2:2–3) so that he
    turns his heart to you!
Through your Word, make him "wise for salvation through faith in
    Christ Jesus" (2 Timothy 3:15).
Help him to be "wise about what is good,
    and innocent about what is evil" (Romans 16:19).

Lord Jesus, just as you "grew in wisdom and stature,
and in favor with God and men" (Luke 2:52),
I ask that my son would grow in you in every way.
Let him shine so brightly with your wisdom that he will
"lead many to righteousness" (Daniel 12:3).
Thank you, Father, that this is a prayer you love to answer!
Thank you that you give wisdom when we ask, because you are the
source of it!
"To the only wise God be glory forever
through Jesus Christ! Amen" (Romans 16:27).

Wonderful Light

But you are a chosen people, a royal priesthood, a holy nation,
a people belonging to God, that you may declare the praises of
him who called you out of darkness into his wonderful light.

1 PETER 2:9

I always leave the light on at night for my son, Father.
That's also what this prayer is about.
I ask for your light to fall upon his path and lead him home.
Let him see your light from the distance and be drawn to you.
Let him praise you because you "called" him
    "out of darkness into" your "wonderful light."
Even though he now sits "in darkness,"
    I ask that you will be his light (Micah 7:8).
I praise you that there is no darkness so black
    that you cannot show him the way out of it.
Bring him to the place where he can say, "You are my lamp, O LORD;
    the LORD turns my darkness into light" (2 Samuel 22:29).
Your light is wonderful, Lord.
You are "the Ancient of Days" (Daniel 7:22).
Day and night, darkness and light have been under your control
    since before time began.
You see in the dark!
Even the "darkness is as light to you" (Psalm 139:12),
    and in you "there is no darkness at all" (1 John 1:5).
You know the way for my son to come home so that he will be a son
    "of the light" and a son "of the day" (1 Thessalonians 5:5)—
    your son!
Then he will "walk in" your light (Isaiah 2:5) in this world and the
    next, until he comes to the city that "does not need the sun
    or the moon to shine on it," because your glory "gives it light"
    (Revelation 21:23).

Be his light and his hope, Lord Jesus! You are "the light of men" (John 1:4)!

Thank you, Father, for shining your light "in the darkness" (John 1:5) and for leaving the light on for my son.

Lead him out of "the dominion of darkness" and "into the kingdom of the Son" you love, "in whom we have redemption, the forgiveness of sins" (Colossians 1:13–14).

Then we will declare your praises together forever (1 Peter 2:9), because you turned our night into everlasting day.

Back to Flame

A bruised reed he will not break, and a smoldering wick
he will not snuff out.

Isaiah 42:3

She had more faith once, Father. Remember?
It was beautiful to see: the simple, heartfelt faith of a child.
She loved you, and the little candle of her faith burned brightly for all
    to see.
But then the winds came.
Even though I tried to shield the flame of her faith from the world's
    incessant blowing, my hands could only do so much.
That's why I'm placing her in your hands again today, Lord Jesus.
I can't imagine anything more fragile than "a smoldering wick."
I thank you that you "will not snuff out" this candle,
    which is my daughter's faith.
Protect and nurture it, Father, so that it will glow brightly once again.
I ask for you to surround her and shield her faith from the world
    (Psalm 5:12).
Rebuke the world's wind and storms the way you did long ago:
    "Quiet! Be still!" (Mark 4:39).
Then she will look on you with awe, just like the disciples did.
I pray you will protect her fragile faith in every way so that she can
    "stand against the devil's schemes" (Ephesians 6:11).
Father, I pray you will send someone she trusts
    to tell her "the good news about Jesus" again (Acts 8:35).
I ask that her heart will be open, and that through your loving
    Spirit, she will receive the good news "with deep conviction"
    (1 Thessalonians 1:5).
I pray that faith will permeate her life in a fresh and bold new way,
    and that she will live it out consistently.
Help her to see that "the kingdom of God is not a matter of talk
    but of power" (1 Corinthians 4:20).

I pray she "may have power, together with all the saints, to grasp how wide and long and high and deep is" your love so that she may be "filled to the measure" of all your fullness (Ephesians 3:18–19).

Then, let her "fan into flame" every gift you've given her so that the candle of her faith will burn brightly once again (2 Timothy 1:6).

Let her shine so brightly that others "can see the light" (Luke 8:16) and come to you!

I praise you, Lord, that in your hands even a smoldering wick can come to life again.

I pray in your name that her faith will burn brightly!

Dressed in Armor

*Put on the full armor of God so that you can take
your stand against the devil's schemes.*

EPHESIANS 6:11

We need to dress my son, Lord. Just like I did when he was little,
   only this time with armor.
Your armor. Armor made especially for him.
He doesn't know how to put it on himself yet,
   so I ask your help to put it on him. He needs it more than he knows.
He's been walking too close to where the enemy walks, and he's in
   danger.
Show him "your ways, O Lord. Teach" him "your paths" (Psalm 25:4).
Help him to "stand firm" in your truth, with the "belt of truth
   buckled" around his waist (Ephesians 6:14).
I pray he will "love the truth and so be saved" (2 Thessalonians 2:10).
I see the "breastplate of righteousness" in your Word, Father
   (Ephesians 6:14).
   Please put it on him.
Just as Abraham believed you, "and it was credited to him as
   righteousness, and he was called" your "friend" (James 2:23),
   I pray my son will believe *you*, Lord Jesus, and know you as
   his friend.
You said, "You are my friends if you do what I command" (John 15:14).
   I pray that he will obey you!
Then let his feet be "fitted with the readiness that comes
   from the gospel of peace" (Ephesians 6:15).
Make him ready to tell others about you.
   Right now he's working on his testimony, he just doesn't know
   it yet!
I "take up the shield of faith," Father,
   to "extinguish all the flaming arrows of the evil one"
   (Ephesians 6:16).

I would step in front of my son if I could,
 and I *do* know that my prayers protect him.
But I also ask that he will learn to use the shield for himself.
In order to do that, he needs to "take the helmet of salvation"
 (Ephesians 6:17), and I pray with all of my heart that he will.
Then give him "the sword of the Spirit,
 which is the word of God" (Ephesians 6:17).
May he love your Word, Lord!
Help him to use it whenever he is tempted, so he may stand his
 ground.
Let him "pray in the Spirit on all occasions with all kinds of prayers
 and requests" (Ephesians 6:18), by having his mind
 "set on what the Spirit desires" (Romans 8:5).
Give him grace to understand the power of prayer and the eternal
 difference it makes in his life and the lives of others.
Please, use this prayer to make a difference in his life today!

When Angels Sing

In the same way, I tell you, there is rejoicing in the presence
of the angels of God over one sinner who repents.

LUKE 15:10

I ask that he will make angels sing, Father.
I pray he will turn from his past and run with an open heart and mind
  to you!
I can imagine the joy.
My joy here on earth would only be part of a much larger celebration,
  because "There is rejoicing in the presence of the angels of God
  over one sinner who repents" (Luke 15:10).
Your Word tells of "thousands upon thousands of angels" joyfully
  praising you (Hebrews 12:22), and so they should!
"You are worthy, our Lord and God, to receive glory and honor and
  power, for you created all things, and by your will they were
  created and have their being" (Revelation 4:11).
You created my son and gave him life.
You long for him with an everlasting love.
You loved him so much that you gave your "one and only Son, that
  whoever believes in him shall not perish but have eternal life"
  (John 3:16).
No wonder the angels sing when one sinner repents!
I pray that my son will know the joy of repentance, Lord.
Not just the joy of the angels or my joy, but especially *yours* and *his*!
You want "everyone to come to repentance" (2 Peter 3:9),
  and welcome him with opens arms as he draws near.
Then, like the father in the story of the prodigal son, you "bring
  the best robe and put it on him" (Luke 15:22)—a robe of
  righteousness!
You throw a party in heaven and the angels sing!
And the joy that you have—your pure, perfect joy—shows up on
  his face.

He is safe and home, "set free from sin" (Romans 6:22) to serve you and love you forever, restored to the joy of a right relationship with you, free at last!

I pray he will give his heart to you soon, Lord!

Then let him make the angels continue to sing by bringing others to you.

I pray that he may be active in sharing his faith, so that he will have "a full understanding of every good thing we have in" you (Philemon 1:6).

I can almost hear the music playing, Father.

Please let it begin for him today!

For the Keeping of Angels

See that you do not look down on one of these little ones.
For I tell you that their angels in heaven always
see the face of my Father in heaven.

MATTHEW 18:10

Your Word says you send your angels to do your "bidding,"
    Father (Psalm 103:20).
Thank you for giving our children angels who "always see" your face.
Thank you for all the times you've looked after my child when I could
    not: the near misses, the fraction-of-a-second, happened-too-fast-
    for-me-to-react moments when your angel intervened.
My child needs the protection of your angels now, Lord.
Just like when you sent one to watch over Daniel
    and "shut the mouths of the lions" (Daniel 6:22).
I need your angels to go where I cannot go, just as you did the nights
    you rescued Peter "from Herod's clutches" (Acts 12:11)
    and "opened the doors of the jail" for the apostles (Acts 5:19).
I know some might think it presumptuous of me to ask for angels for
    someone who is not where he's supposed to be, but you've done
    this before.
You did it for Elijah when he "was afraid and ran for his life"
    (1 Kings 19:3). "All at once an angel touched him," not once,
    but twice (1 Kings 19:5, 7).
You also had your angels take Lot's hand "when he hesitated" to leave
    Sodom with his family, because you were "merciful to them"
    (Genesis 19:16).
You are merciful, Lord! And you said that "whatever you loose on
    earth will be loosed in heaven" (Matthew 18:18).
So I ask that you send an angel from heaven to help my son.
Just as "some people have entertained angels without knowing it"
    (Hebrews 13:2), let a stranger show him a kindness that he knows
    is from you.

Or, as when you sent your angels to shepherds with the "good news" of Jesus (Luke 2:10), send someone to share your love and your presence with him so that he will believe, seek you out, and bow before you.

You've said that "the angel of the Lord encamps around those who fear him, and he delivers them" (Psalm 34:7).

Because I "know what it is to fear" you (2 Corinthians 5:11), Lord, with reverence, awe, and love, I ask that you deliver my son.

Your Word tells me about what you've done for those you call your own: "In all their distress he too was distressed, and the angel of his presence saved them. In his love and mercy he redeemed them" (Isaiah 63:9).

Redeem my son, Lord! Let him be a joy to you and to all of heaven, because "there is rejoicing in the presence of the angels of God over one sinner who repents" (Luke 15:10).

I don't know how you will do it, but I ask you to help him open his heart to you.

I'd love to know how you're going to do it, Lord, but I know that "even angels long to look into these things" (1 Peter 1:12).

So I will watch and pray and wait, and say with the angels, "Praise and glory and wisdom and thanks and honor and power and strength be to our God for ever and ever. Amen!" (Revelation 7:11–12).

Quiet in His Love

The Lord your God is with you, he is mighty to save. He will take great delight in you, he will quiet you with his love, he will rejoice over you with singing.

ZEPHANIAH 3:17

"The Lord your God is with you, he is mighty to save. He will take
   great delight in you, he will quiet you with his love, he will rejoice
   over you with singing."
What beautiful thoughts, Lord.
You are all of those things!
You *are* "with [me]."
You *are* "mighty to save."
The thought of you taking delight in me and comforting me with your
   love gives my soul hope that this world cannot take away.
When I imagine you rejoicing over me with singing, I'm reminded
   that you are my Father, and I am your child (1 John 5:19).
"How great is the love the Father has lavished on us, that we should
   be called children of God! And that is what we are!" (1 John 3:1).
When my daughter was little, Father, I *rejoiced* over her with singing.
There were lullabies and happy songs, and quiet moments just
   between us.
How good it was just to hold her in my arms
   and feel the softness of her cheek next to mine.
What a gift she was, Father, and still is!
Even though she has made choices that have grieved me and grieved
   you, I cannot give up on her.
I will "keep on praying" (Ephesians 6:18) until she is restored to a
   right relationship with you.
Then when she comes home to you, I will pray some more,
   praising you for what you have done!
In the "quietness and confidence" that comes from you alone (Isaiah
   32:17), I will wait and watch and pray.

You are "the God who gives endurance and encouragement" (Romans 15:5).

Your love will go the distance to bring her home.

Let it happen soon, Lord!

I can hardly wait to see her face reflecting your love and goodness and grace, because you make your "face shine upon" her (Numbers 6:25).

Because of your kindness and mercy I "do not lose heart" (2 Corinthians 4:1).

I'm lifted by the vision of *you* being with her, taking "great delight" in her, quieting her with your love, and rejoicing over her "with singing."

You *are* "mighty to save," Father!

All of my hope is in you.

Who Sinned?

*His disciples asked him, "Rabbi, who sinned, this man
or his parents, that he was born blind?"*

JOHN 9:2

One Saturday afternoon, when my sister came home from college, she went out to lunch at a local restaurant with Dad. They were holding hands across the table and talking intently when the phone rang at home.

My mother answered the phone. It was a lady from our church.

"Mrs. Banks, do you know where your husband is right now? It is my Christian duty to inform you that he is having lunch with some blond *thing*."

Mom, who knew exactly where Dad was, decided to play along: "Is he doing that again?"

"You mean he's done it before?"

"Oh, yes. Thank you for telling me. Good-bye."

That was the end of the conversation.

The next morning, Mom had the family wait on the church's front steps after worship. When the woman who had called her came out the front doors, Mom pointed to my sister and said with a smile, "I'd like to introduce you to my daughter."

Have you ever jumped to conclusions without knowing all of the facts? That's what the disciples were doing when they encountered a blind man and asked Jesus, "Rabbi, who sinned, this man or his parents, that he was born blind?"

God promises in His Word that "the son will not share the guilt of the father, nor will the father share the guilt of the son" (Ezekiel 18:20). But as the disciples' question demonstrated, many in Jesus' day believed that sickness was the direct result of sin either in the life of the one who was ill or his parents.

Jesus' response to the disciples speaks volumes: "Neither this man nor his parents sinned . . . but this happened so that the work of God might be displayed in his life" (John 9:3). While the disciples were busy looking for sin and someone to blame, Jesus saw an opportunity to show the greatness and the love of God. Sometimes the parents of prodigals may find themselves thinking like the disciples. We look for someone to blame, and don't look very far. More than one parent of a prodigal son or daughter has found themselves asking, "Is God punishing me through my child for something I did in the past?" Fortunately, Jesus' response to the disciples and God's promise through Ezekiel indicate that the answer to that question is an emphatic "No."

God's promise through Ezekiel makes it clear that each of us must take responsibility for our own actions. We cannot blame parents or genetics for our sins. We also cannot blame ourselves for the sinful choices of a son or daughter. Still, that's not always easy.

There have been times when I've heard my parents' words coming out of my mouth when I talk to my children (the words *"Because I said so!"* come to mind). I've also heard the words I spoke to my parents coming out of my children's mouths. When those words are hurtful, I've caught myself thinking, "This sounds *too* familiar. Is my past coming back to haunt me? Is God judging me for my own rebellion by giving me a rebellious child? Is this my *payback*?"

Thankfully, God doesn't see it that way. His promise is worth repeating and taking to heart: "The son will not share the guilt of the father." I take great comfort in that, because I don't want my children to bear the burden of things I did long ago. It's also good to know that God isn't holding them against me.

The spiritual blindness in our children's lives is not caused by sins of the parents but by sin that is part of the fallen nature we all share, because "all have sinned and fall short of the glory of God" (Romans 3:23). That sin has consequences, and we must repent of it and leave it at the foot of the cross. But before that can happen for our prodigal children, Jesus must open their eyes.

It's encouraging that Jesus came of his own initiative to the man who was blind from birth. The man didn't ask for Jesus' help. Jesus sought *him* out. He *stopped* and looked the man in his sightless eyes.

Jesus is also able to encounter our children when they are not looking for Him. God has ways of reaching our children that we've never thought of. Jesus loves our prodigal kids and wants to display the work of God in their lives, no matter what they've done. "God demonstrates his own love for us in this: While we were still sinners, Christ died for us" (Romans 5:8). Jesus wants to touch our children and set them free, so they will become witnesses to the Father's kindness and power, and one day love others into the kingdom.

Our prodigals don't know it yet, but right now they're just working on their testimonies.

Jesus is coming their way, and someday they will tell of all he has done for them, just like another young man long ago. One day, "the eyes" of their hearts will "be enlightened" (Ephesians 1:18) and his words will be theirs: "One thing I do know. I was blind but now I see!" (John 9:25).

There is no place where earth's sorrows
are more felt than up in heaven;
there is no place where earth's failings
have such kindly judgment given.

Frederick W. Faber, "There's a Wideness in God's Mercy"

Sins of the Parents?

As he went along, he saw a man blind from birth.
His disciples asked him, "Rabbi, who sinned, this man
or his parents, that he was born blind?"

JOHN 9:1–2

Sometimes I feel like asking the same question that was on the mind
of the disciples, Lord: "Who sinned? This man or his parents?"
At times I've wondered if the spiritual blindness in my son's life
is because of some sin I committed in the past.
Thank you, Father, that you don't see it that way at all.
There was a time when you would punish "the children for the sin of
the fathers to the third and fourth generation" (Numbers 14:18),
but no longer.
You've done something entirely new!
You promise in your Word that "the son will not share the guilt
of the father, nor will the father share the guilt of the son."
You say that you will judge "each one according to his ways."
Thank you, Father, that through your mercy we can have
"a new heart and a new spirit" (Ezekiel 18:20, 30–31).
I understand that we are all "born blind," because through Adam's sin,
"sin entered the world" (Romans 5:12),
and "all have sinned and fall short" of your glory (Romans 3:23).
"There is no one righteous, not even one" (Romans 3:10).
But you promise, "I will give you a new heart and put a new spirit
in you."
You even say, "I will put *my Spirit* in you
and move you to follow my decrees" (Ezekiel 36:26–27).
I praise you that you opened for us "a new and living way" (Hebrews
10:20) through your Son!
You have "given us the Spirit as a deposit,
guaranteeing what is to come" (2 Corinthians 5:5)!

Thank you that your Word assures us, "The promise is for you and your children and for all who are far off—for all whom the Lord our God will call" (Acts 2:39)!

My child is far off, Lord, just like I was. Please call him.

Let him hear your voice beckoning him to come home.

I praise you that you "do not hold against us the sins of the fathers" (Psalm 79:8).

"With you there is forgiveness" (Psalm 130:4)!

Though we are born spiritually blind, in your mercy you touch us and open our eyes so that we can "see wonderful things" (Psalm 119:18).

Just as you did for that young man who was born "blind from birth," I ask that you look on my son with your love and compassion.

Oh Lord, please let my son see the wonder of all that you are today!

Strength to Go On

Though the fig tree does not bud and there are no grapes on the vines, though the olive crop fails and the fields produce no food, though there are no sheep in the pen and no cattle in the stalls, yet I will rejoice in the LORD, I will be joyful in God my Savior.

HABAKKUK 3:17–19

I will remind myself of this, Lord:
    It's always good to praise you, regardless of how I feel at the moment.
"For great is the LORD and most worthy of praise" (1 Chronicles 16:25).
"I *will* rejoice in the LORD. I *will* be joyful in God" (Habakkuk 3:18),
    regardless of my external circumstances on any given day.
    And *why not?*
Yes, times are difficult with my child. She's running from me
    and from you.
My heart aches. I long to take her in my arms and protect her from
    harm, if only she would have it.
Then I am reminded of your Word and your promise:
    "Yet the LORD longs to be gracious to you;
    he rises to show you compassion" (Isaiah 30:18).
There's a lot of meaning in that one word, *yet.* You know how I feel,
    don't you?
Not only about my daughter. About the whole human race.
That's why you came, why you sent *your* one and only son:
    "We all, like sheep, have gone astray, each of us has turned to
    his own way; and the LORD has laid on him the iniquity of us all"
    (Isaiah 53:6).
Not only do you understand, you've faced our rebellion with a heart
    that feels with more "depth" than I could ever know
    (Romans 11:33).
I praise you for that and will wait for you, because "since ancient
    times no one has heard, no ear has perceived, no eye has seen any

God besides you, who acts on behalf of those who wait for him" (Isaiah 64:4).

Even though my daughter is far away from you right now, "surely the arm of the LORD is not too short to save" (Isaiah 59:1).

You *want* to draw her close. You have told us in your Word that "the promise is for you and your children and for all who are far off—for all whom the Lord our God will call" (Acts 2:39).

I hold on to that promise, and I hold on to you.

I choose to praise you and hope in you because it's the best course of action and you deserve it. And you bless us all the more when we trust in you.

"Those who hope in the LORD will renew their strength" (Isaiah 40:31).

"Blessed are those who have learned to acclaim you" (Psalm 89:15).

"Blessed are those whose strength is in you" (Psalm 84:5)!

I am blessed, Lord. You are my blessing!

And I praise you for *you*, with all my heart!

How Long, O Lord?

How long, O Lord, how long?

PSALM 6:3

I've heard it said that I shouldn't pray for patience, Lord,
    and that if I ask for patience I'm only asking for difficulty.
I don't want to believe that it always works that way.
Better put, I don't want to believe that you always work that way.
Your Word tells me that "the Lord is good to those whose hope is
    in him, to the one who seeks him" (Lamentations 3:25).
I do hope in you, and I am seeking you this morning once again.
I know that you are faithful and that you answer prayer.
But right now I'd like to ask you (just like David did),
    "How long, O Lord?"
Your Word promises, "Ask and it will be given to you; seek,
    and you will find; knock and the door will be opened to you"
    (Matthew 7:7).
Still, sometimes I feel like I've been asking and seeking and knocking
    at that door for days on end and it still stays shut and locked.
Now is one of those times. I feel stuck between 'how it is and how it
    could be.'
I'd love to see a change in my child's heart and life, and I do trust that
    you will make that happen, but it hasn't happened yet.
I don't want to sound like I'm "complaining," Father (Philippians 2:14),
    or to be like those who grumbled against you in the wilderness
    (Numbers 14:29).
You know my heart completely as I come to you in prayer
    (2 Chronicles 6:30). You know that what I'm doing is *longing.*
"I long for your salvation, O Lord" (Psalm 119:174).
I long to see my son's heart filled with the joy you alone can give
    (Psalm 4:7).
I long to see him "turn from evil and do good" (Psalm 34:14).

Like the father who saw his prodigal coming home "while he was still a long way off" (Luke 15:20), I'm watching and waiting.

I'm "looking for your salvation" (Psalm 119:123).

My "eyes look to the LORD our God, till he shows us his mercy" (Psalm 123:2).

Lord Jesus, just like others who called out to you before and kept calling until an answer came, I'm crying out to you: "Lord, Son of David, have mercy on us!" (Matthew 20:30–31).

I'm placing all of my hope in you and asking for the patience to keep hoping, keep watching, keep calling . . . no matter how long it takes.

I praise you in advance for the day your purpose will be fulfilled in my son's life.

I praise you for the day he and I will say together, "Today salvation has come to this house . . . For the Son of Man came to seek and to save what was lost" (Luke 19:9–10).

When You're "Prayed Out"

Who is he that condemns? Christ Jesus, who died—
more than that, who was raised to life—is at the
right hand of God and is also interceding for us.

ROMANS 8:34

Sometimes I feel too numb to pray, Father.
It's not that I don't believe you answer prayer. I do believe.
But sometimes when I pray and pray and don't see any change
    in my child, I lose heart.
Please forgive my lack of faith and impatience, Lord.
Help me to take your Word to heart, that we "should always pray
    and not give up" (Luke 18:1).
When the woman kept knocking on the door of the "unjust judge"
    (Luke 18:6), she got what she asked for.
When the Canaanite woman pleaded with you for her daughter,
    and the disciples tried to send her away,
    you *did* grant the woman's request (Matthew 15:25–28).
When the man knocked on his friend's door after midnight,
    and the friend wanted him to go away,
    you said "because of the man's boldness he will get up
    and give him as much as he needs" (Luke 11:8).
Help me to be bold, Lord! Especially now!
My daughter needs me to be, and I know you want me to be.
I want to thank you that you help me to pray.
    I especially need that help right now.
Thank you that you are "at the right hand" of the Father,
    "interceding for us" (Romans 8:34).
Holy Spirit, I praise you that you are praying for me and my child
    "with groans that words cannot express" (Romans 8:26).
Lord Jesus, I thank you that when my faith is lacking,
    you "will remain faithful" (2 Timothy 2:13).

I praise you that "faith as small as a mustard seed" can move
    mountains (Matthew 17:20). I have that!

My faith may be small right now, but it's enough when I place it in
    your hands.

So I place my daughter in your hands again, no matter how
    challenging things may be.

You said it yourself: "What is impossible with men is possible with
    God" (Luke 18:27), and "all things are possible with God"
    (Mark 10:27).

I hold on to those promises right now, and praise you that "no matter
    how many promises God has made, they are 'Yes' in Christ"
    (2 Corinthians 1:20).

I will keep coming to you, Lord, and keep praying. How can I not?

Your "Yes!" is all I need.

When He Is Older

Train a child in the way he should go,
and when he is old he will not turn from it.

PROVERBS 22:6

I can see him years from now, Father. When my prayers have been
   answered, and his heart has turned to you.

I can see him standing strong, "a good man, full of the Holy Spirit and
   faith" (Acts 11:24).

For that to happen, I know I need to do my best to
   build a "firm foundation" (1 Timothy 6:19) for him, Father.

Of all of the things I may do for my child, I understand that nothing is
   more important than sharing your love with him, not just "with
   words or tongue but with actions and in truth" (1 John 3:18).

Even though this is a challenging time in his life, help me to
   "be prepared in season and out of season" so that I may
   "correct, rebuke and encourage—with great patience
   and careful instruction" (2 Timothy 4:2).

I praise you for the truth that if I raise him "in the way he should go,"
   "when he is old he will not turn from it."

I want to help him "take hold of the life that is truly life"
   (1 Timothy 6:19).

Let him be spared the pain and difficulty of years lived apart from
   you, and give his heart to you soon!

You tell us we "must be ready," because you "will come at an hour
   when" we "do not expect" (Matthew 24:44).

I pray he *will* be ready and will give his heart to you today!

You promise that your Word will not return to you empty, "but will
   accomplish what" you "desire and achieve the purpose for which"
   you "sent it" (Isaiah 55:11).

I pray that you will help me as I communicate your Word and your
   love to my son.

Help me to make the good news of Jesus as clear to him as I
   possibly can.
Give him "ears to hear" your Word as I share it with him
   so that he truly listens (Mark 4:9).
Let him not only "listen to the word," but help him to "do what it
   says" and follow you in obedience and love (James 1:22).
I love my son, Lord, and I thank you for entrusting him to me.
I know you have given him to me so that I may point him to you.
You are "the God who gives life to the dead and calls things that are
   not as though they were" (Romans 4:17).
I pray you will raise him to life in you and call him your own!
I can see the day coming by faith when he's "filled to the measure
   of all the fullness" you want to give him (Ephesians 3:19).
And I praise you because you are "faithful,"
   and you "will do it" (1 Thessalonians 5:24).

When Sorrow and Sighing Flee Away

And the ransomed of the LORD will return. They will enter Zion
with singing; everlasting joy will crown their heads. Gladness and
joy will overtake them, and sorrow and sighing will flee away.

ISAIAH 35:10

What a day that will be, Lord!
The day that my daughter comes home to you,
    ransomed, forgiven, restored, and blessed.
I can almost hear her singing!
I long for your "everlasting joy" to crown her
    and for her to find 'soul satisfaction' in you!
I can imagine what the day will be like, Lord.
I can see your "gladness and joy" keeping pace behind her,
    getting closer and closer until they completely overtake her
    and she finds the desire of her heart in you.
I can also see "sorrow and sighing" flee away as each of the world's
    hurts and deceptions are scattered "in the light of your presence"
    (Psalm 90:8), and the truth and beauty of all that you are "shines
    forth" (Psalm 50:2).
I praise you, Father, for what you will do.
I pray that even now you will prepare my daughter's heart for it:
    remove every resistance, overcome every argument, expose every
    allure and false affection until she comes to understand that you
    are her deepest need and greatest hope.
Let nothing hold her back, Lord!
You said, "whatever you loose on earth will be loosed in heaven"
    (Matthew 16:19).
Release her from every constraint that keeps her from coming to you.
Let loose every blessing you have waiting that will draw her heart
    to you.
You say in your perfect wisdom, "I love those who love me,
    and those who seek me find me" (Proverbs 8:17).

Let her seek you, find you, and love you, Lord!

I praise you, Lord Jesus, that you came to give your life as a ransom for many (Mark 10:45).

I pray with all my heart that my daughter will be among the ransomed who sing for joy as they return to you!

More than I Ask or Imagine

*Now to him who is able to do immeasurably more than all
we ask or imagine, according to his power that is at work
within us, to him be glory in the church and in Christ Jesus
throughout all generations, for ever and ever! Amen.*

EPHESIANS 3:20–21

I can imagine the difference you will make in my son's life
on the day he comes back to you.
But I praise you that no matter what I'm looking forward to,
you are "able to do *immeasurably more* than all" I "ask or
imagine."
Thank you, Almighty Father, for "things too wonderful for me
to know" (Job 42:3).
My prayer is that my son will be among the "generations" who praise
you "for ever and ever," but you can even do more than that! You
can even use him to lead others to you!
You are "wonderful in counsel and magnificent in wisdom"
(Isaiah 28:29)!
"I am your servant" (1 Kings 18:36), Lord. I want to serve you in any
way you want in order to help my son draw closer to you.
I ask that you "give me discernment" for whatever you desire
(Psalm 119:125).
I pray that you will convict him of any sin in his life
that holds him back from coming to you.
I pray that he will be "cleansed from his past sins" (2 Peter 1:9) by
confessing them to you and finding mercy through "the blood of
Jesus" that "purifies us from all sin" (1 John 1:7).
Let him understand deeply in his heart that you sent Jesus to save
him, because "if anyone acknowledges that Jesus is the Son of
God," you will live "in him and he in" you (1 John 4:15).
Father, because you gave your son to me and held nothing back,
I give my son to you.

It is only right, because he was your gift to me to begin with.

"Every living soul belongs to" you (Ezekiel 18:4).

Revive my son, Lord! Breathe the breath of eternal life into his soul.

"This is eternal life: that" he "may know you, the only true God, and Jesus Christ, whom you have sent" (John 17:3).

"Many, O LORD my God, are the wonders you have done" (Psalm 40:5).

Do another, Father! I pray not only that my son will come to life in you today, but that you would not stop there!

Do "immeasurably more" because "nothing is too hard for you" (Jeremiah 32:17)!

The Good Shepherd

The Pharisees and the teachers of the law muttered, "This man welcomes sinners and eats with them." Then Jesus told them this parable: "Suppose one of you has a hundred sheep and loses one of them. Does he not leave the ninety-nine in the open country and go after the lost sheep until he finds it? And when he finds it, he joyfully puts it on his shoulders and goes home. Then he calls his friends and neighbors together and says, 'Rejoice with me; I have found my lost sheep.' I tell you that in the same way there will be more rejoicing in heaven over one sinner who repents than over ninety-nine righteous persons who do not need to repent."

LUKE 15:2–7

It's a long road between Amarillo and Albuquerque. Especially when your kids are at that "are we there yet?" age.

But this was a quiet moment. Bryan was asleep (finally!), Cari was driving, and Katie and I were in the backseat, watching the lines go by on the pavement.

Katie doesn't sleep much in the car. She gets that from me. Cari and Bryan can zonk out anywhere. Katie and I are wired differently.

It was the middle of the morning. We had started early to beat the desert heat. Cari tried to be helpful: "Why don't you two just close your eyes and go to sleep?"

She could just as easily have told us to strap ourselves to the roof rack—we were as wide-eyed as if we had done just that. We had gone through all of Katie's books, played with her Barbies, and sung every song we could remember. But I-40 was merciless. It just kept going in one . . . straight . . . very long . . . line.

Then Katie came up with a new idea.

"Daddy, will you tell me a story?"

Katie loved my stories, and she knew I loved telling them to her. Suddenly the ride became interesting for both of us. The stories came in rapid succession.

"Tell me another!"

On and on it went, until Dad's creative well began to run dry. "I can't think of anything else right now, Katie."

"Are you sure? C'mon, Dad! Just one more! Don't you know any other stories?"

"Well, there is one. And it isn't just any story. It's the best story of all, because it's true."

I had shared the good news about Jesus with Katie several times before, but this time was different. I sensed that she was grasping the words and taking them to heart, and God was enabling me to explain the gospel with a clarity that could have come only from Him. His Spirit was at work. I could feel it.

I explained the story of salvation to her from creation to Easter, and she listened intently. When I asked her if she believed it was true, she nodded her head. When I asked, "Would you like to ask Jesus to come into your heart and take your sins away?" her response was an immediate "Yes!"

We bowed our heads and she began to pray with words that were simple but sincere. It was a precious moment that I will remember as long as I live. Cari and I understood in that moment that God was doing something very special in our daughter's life, even in her tender years.

Sometimes that moment seems like a lifetime ago, even though it was only a little over a decade. Katie is in college now, and the choices she made during adolescence were sometimes heartbreaking. Some nights we were reminded of what a friend—a church planter like myself (i.e., a pastor who starts a new church)—had told us: "Being a church planter is like painting a target on your back and saying to the devil, 'Come get me.'" In our instance, the devil went after both of our children.

But he's not the only one who is going after them. Not only are Cari and I pursuing them with our prayers, we're doing our best to keep up with the Good Shepherd as he takes strides to bring them back to the fold.

Jesus' parable of the lost sheep in Luke 15:1–7 is just as much about the shepherd as it is about the sheep. He feels such a sense of loss when he discovers that he's missing a sheep that he leaves ninety-nine sheep in "open country" to go after one. "And when he finds it, he joyfully puts it on his shoulders and goes home." Then he calls his friends and throws a party. Jesus wraps up the parable by saying, "I tell you that in the same way there will be more rejoicing in heaven over one sinner who repents than over ninety-nine righteous persons who do not need to repent."

That kind of joy tells me something. The Good Shepherd won't give up looking, even if it takes a lifetime. Though the way is long and hard and uphill, He'll persevere. He knows where His sheep are, and He will find the way to them.

So must do our best to stay close to Him while the search continues. When He will bring them home, we do not know. We just know that He's looking. And that should give us the hope we need to go on.

Even though His sheep has strayed, he or she could be close, just over the next hill. The Good Shepherd knows, and He has a way of surprising us.

I've seen His work before.

Heading west on I-40, I saw the badlands open out into Promised Land.

The answer to our prayers could be just around the bend.

Do not be afraid, for I am with you; I will bring your children from the east and gather you from the west. I will say to the north, "Give them up!" and to the south, "Do not hold them back."

Isaiah 43:5–6

Your Dream for My Child

And afterward, I will pour out my Spirit on all people.
Your sons and daughters will prophesy, your old men will
dream dreams, your young men will see visions.

JOEL 2:28

Father, you have a vision for my child that is beautiful beyond words.
You are "wonderful in counsel and magnificent in wisdom"
    (Isaiah 28:29).
I can only imagine what you have planned for her!
I have so many dreams for my child, Father.
I believe I want good things for her. But my wisdom is limited,
    and my heart has been tainted by sin.
So I want what you want, Lord. Your vision for her, your dream
    for her future!
There is no sin in you (1 John 3:5). Your way is perfect
    (2 Samuel 22:31).
You have promised, "Call to me and I will answer you and tell you
    great and unsearchable things you do not know" (Jeremiah 33:3).
I do call to you for her, and thank you that you will answer.
It's not so much that I need to know your vision for her life
    as *she needs to know it.*
She needs to "taste and see" that you are good (Psalm 34:8).
She needs to know that you are "a refuge in times of trouble,"
    and that you care for "those who trust" in you (Nahum 1:7).
She has an adversary that you know better than I, even though
    "we are not unaware of his schemes" (2 Corinthians 2:11).
Father, I ask in the strong name of Jesus that you frustrate every plan
    that the enemy has against my daughter.
I long to see your Spirit bless my child, Father, while she is still young.
Let her be happy in you, and let her heart give her joy and the wisdom
    to know that she will one day stand before you.

She needs to acknowledge you in all her ways so that you will make her "paths straight" (Proverbs 3:6) and keep her "from the snares" (Proverbs 14:27) that would bring her harm.

Lord Jesus, I pray that she will learn from you, for you are "gentle and humble in heart."

In you, she will "find rest" for her soul (Matthew 11:29).

Be her rest, Lord, and her "peace" (Ephesians 2:14).

Be her life and her purpose, her ultimate goal. This is your dream for my child.

"Blessed is" she "whose help is the God of Jacob,
    whose hope is in the LORD" (Psalm 146:5).

Oh, Lord, be her help and her hope!

Father, please give my daughter grace to turn to you!

Turning Hearts

He will turn the hearts of the fathers to their children,
and the hearts of the children to their fathers.

MALACHI 4:6

Thank you, Lord, for turning my heart to my son.
What a blessing it is to pray for him! I'm grateful for both the privilege
    and the opportunity to see you move in his life in answer to
    prayer.
As I pray, I'm reminded of how much you love him, and of the truth
    that "there is a future hope" for him that "will not be cut off"
    (Proverbs 24:14) because of your kindness.
Father, I'd like to ask you to turn his heart as well.
"Let him turn to the LORD, and he will have mercy on him,
    and to our God, for he will freely pardon" (Isaiah 55:7).
Father, the thought of being separated from my son for all eternity
    is more than I can bear.
He must come to you, Father! You are "God who saves" (Psalm 68:20).
Please save him! Fill him "with all joy and peace" as he trusts in you
    (Romans 15:13). Let it happen today!
I pray that you will strengthen him with power through your Spirit
    in his inner being "so that Christ may dwell" in his heart through
    faith (Ephesians 3:17).
Father, as you move in his heart in a special way,
    I'd also like to ask that you turn his heart to me.
The past years have been difficult and have sometimes caused
    distance between us.
Father, you can find the way to get through to his heart
    and to let him know how much I love him.
I choose to forgive him for what has happened in the past, Lord,
    just as you have forgiven me (Colossians 3:13).

Please help him also to "get rid of all bitterness" (Ephesians 4:31) toward me, so that nothing will mar the love that we have for each other, or for you.

Lord Jesus, long ago you prayed that all who believe in you "may be one" (John 17:11).

I pray that one day my son and I will have "the same love, being one in spirit and purpose" (Philippians 2:2).

I pray that he will be "convinced that neither death nor life, neither angels nor demons, neither the present nor the future, nor any powers, neither height nor depth, nor anything else in all creation, will be able to separate us from the love of God that is in Christ Jesus our Lord" (Romans 8:38–39).

"We are more than conquerors through him who loved us" (Romans 8:37).

Your love conquers all, Lord. Conquer our hearts for you!

The Contender

But this is what the LORD says: "Yes, captives will be taken from warriors, and plunder retrieved from the fierce; I will contend with those who contend with you, and your children I will save."

Isaiah 49:25

We've been contended with, Lord.
The enemy has assaulted my family fiercely and taken my child
    "captive to do his will" (2 Timothy 2:26).
He has sent his fierce warriors to plunder my home and my hopes for
    my child, but he will not succeed.
He has tried to steal that which belongs to *you*.
You made him, and I've given him to you.
Go after the enemy, Lord! "Contend with those who contend with" us!
Take back what is rightfully yours!
You told your people once, "Your children I will save."
Save my son, Father!
I pray that he will come to his "senses and escape from the trap of the
    devil" (2 Timothy 2:26).
Wake him up in the enemy's camp
    and "provide a way out" (1 Corinthians 10:13).
Unlock the chains on his hands and his feet and his heart, and let him
    run to you!
Your Word tells me that you will pursue your "foes into darkness.
    Whatever they plot against the LORD,"
    you "will bring to an end" (Nahum 1:8–9).
I'm counting on that, Father. I'm counting on you!
I ask you to bring back my son and all that has been stolen from us.
Strike down the enemy and bring this matter to a firm and final end.
I can see my son returning to you, held up by your strong arms,
    a captive "set free from sin" (Romans 6:18)!
May he be among those who listen to your voice and "follow you."

You "give them eternal life,
and "no one can snatch them out of"
your hand (John 10:27–28).
I pray my son will be brought into the safety of your love, Lord Jesus.
"The wicked bend their bows; they set their arrows against the strings
to shoot from the shadows" (Psalm 11:2).
But I "take up the shield of faith, with which you can extinguish
all the flaming arrows of the evil one" (Ephesians 6:16).
"Thanks be to" you, Father!
You give us "the victory through our Lord Jesus Christ"
(1 Corinthians 15:57).
Let that victory come in my son's life today!

Running to Jesus

The name of the LORD is a strong tower;
the righteous run to it and are safe.

PROVERBS 18:10

"How sweet the Name of Jesus sounds in a believer's ear!
    It soothes his sorrows, heals his wounds, and drives away
    his fear."[1]
Yes! Your name is sweet to me, Lord!
"Salvation is found in no one else, for there is no other name under
    heaven given to men by which we must be saved" (Acts 4:12).
I pray your name over my child today, Jesus.
There is power in your name! I call upon all that you are to bless my
    son and draw him to you.
I pray that you will be his Wonderful Counselor (Isaiah 9:6)
    who speaks to him of his need for you.
I pray you will be his "good shepherd," that he will know you and
    listen to your voice (John 10:11, 14, 16).
I pray your "goodness and love will follow" him all the days of his life,
    and he will dwell in your house forever (Psalm 23:6).
I ask you to be with him wherever he goes, because you are
    "Immanuel . . . 'God with us'" (Matthew 1:23).
You are "the Lamb of God, who takes away the sin of the world" (John
    1:29), and I plead your mercy for him.
You are "the atoning sacrifice for our sins,"
    the "one who speaks to the Father in our defense" (1 John 2:1–2).
You are "The LORD Our Righteousness" (Jeremiah 23:6).
I pray you will one day be all of these things to my son, and more!
I pray that he will come to you and believe, so that you will be the
    "bread of life" to him, and he will "never go hungry"
    and "never be thirsty" (John 6:35).

---

1. Newton, "How Sweet the Name of Jesus Sounds," *Olney Hymns*, 58.

You are "the author of life" (Acts 3:15). I ask for a new start in life for him, in which you will be "the Alpha and the Omega, the First and the Last, the Beginning and the End" (Revelation 22:13).

Be the "bright Morning Star" (Revelation 22:16)
that rises in his heart (2 Peter 1:19)!

I ask that you will be "the hope of glory" to him (Colossians 1:27), living in him and showing him all of the good things of God.

I pray he will be "made strong" by faith in your name, Lord Jesus (Acts 3:16)!

God has given you "the name that is above every name," that at your name "every knee should bow, in heaven and on earth and under the earth, and every tongue confess" that you are Lord (Philippians 2:9–11).

Let him run to you, Lord, and bow his knees and his heart.

I ask that he will confess that you are Lord, call on your name, and "be saved" (Acts 2:21)!

Inner Beauty

Your beauty should not come from outward adornment, such as
braided hair and the wearing of gold jewelry and fine clothes.
Instead, it should be that of your inner self, the unfading beauty of
a gentle and quiet spirit, which is of great worth in God's sight.

1 Peter 3:3–4

Everywhere she turns she feels the pressure to be beautiful, Father.
The magazines and airwaves call out to her with pitches and promises,
> but the beauty they sell is only skin-deep.
The runways show off styles that sparkle for a season,
> and then end up in a thrift store.
Because even Solomon with all of his wisdom was led "astray"
> by pretty faces (1 Kings 11:3), she needs your wisdom, Lord.
Help her to see through the thin layer of skin to the heart of the matter:
> "Charm is deceptive, and beauty is fleeting;
> > but a woman who fears the Lord is to be praised"
> (Proverbs 31:30).
Father, I pray you will turn her eyes from the world and direct them
> to you.
Then she "will look and be radiant," and her "heart will throb and
> swell with joy" (Isaiah 60:5), because there is no happiness like
> the joy you give!
I ask that you will give her that which matters much to you:
> "the unfading beauty of a gentle and quiet spirit."
Help her to value *inward* adornment over "outward adornment."
Let her be "clothed with strength and dignity" (Proverbs 31:25).
May her soul be "stilled and quieted" as she rests in you (Psalm 131:2).
May your light and love shine from behind her eyes, Lord Jesus,
> because you dwell in her heart "through faith" (Ephesians 3:17).
May her inner beauty be so evident
> that it becomes the first thing others notice about her.
May it be your blessing to draw them to youself through her!

Father, I pray you will protect her from the "meaningless"
(Ecclesiastes 11:10) vanity of this world, which places an
inordinate value on youthful beauty.
Let her know that she is valued by you
and that your opinion matters more than any other.
That way, she will know she is always loved.
Let her "say with confidence, 'The Lord is my helper'" (Hebrews 13:6).
Let her be "filled with an inexpressible and glorious joy" because she
is "receiving the goal" of her faith,
"the salvation" of her soul (1 Peter 1:8–9).
I pray she will place her hope in you, so that the wonder of all that
you are will make her beautiful in every way (1 Peter 3:5),
a shining beauty, from the inside out.

Every Blessing

Every good and perfect gift is from above,
coming down from the Father of the heavenly lights,
who does not change like shifting shadows.

JAMES 1:17

How blessed I am, Father!
You've given me "every spiritual blessing in Christ" (Ephesians 1:3).
Every blessing! Teach me how to count those blessings, Lord,
    and to take so much joy in them that I increasingly
    set my heart "on things above" (Colossians 3:1).
Thank you for the assurance you give that we are your children
    (Romans 8:16).
Thank you for the gift of your Spirit, "freely given" to me
    (1 Corinthians 2:12).
Thank you for the "surpassing greatness" of knowing You, Jesus,
    for you are the greatest blessing of all (Philippians 3:8)!
"Every spiritual blessing"! I'm "an heir" to everything good
    (Galatians 4:7), even though I'm entirely unworthy of it.
How amazing you are to love me and die for me.
You demonstrated your love for me when you were the furthest thing
    from my mind (Romans 5:8).
Father, just as you've had mercy on me and blessed me beyond
    imagination, I'd like to ask for your mercy and blessing for
    my child.
Just as "Isaac blessed Jacob and Esau in regard to their future"
    (Hebrews 11:20), I'd like to ask for future blessings for my son.
I ask that he will be transformed by the renewing of his mind
    to know you and love you (Romans 12:2).
Change his mind and heart with your "treasures of wisdom and
    knowledge" (Colossians 2:3) so that he wants you more than
    anything else.

Touch his stubborn will with your "perfect love" that drives out fear (1 John 4:18).

May your peace, "which transcends all understanding" (Philippians 4:7), rest upon him as he turns his back on the world and draws near to you.

I know you want to bless him too, Father!

Let him live in such a way that he may be truly blessed by you.

"As a father has compassion on his children,
so the LORD has compassion on those who fear him" (Psalm 103:13).

Thank you for the blessing of your compassion and love, Lord Jesus.

I praise you, because you "have overcome the world" (John 16:33).

You are "God who saves" (Psalm 68:20).

Bless him with your salvation, Lord, just like you have blessed me.

Then together we will "praise you forever;
from generation to generation" (Psalm 79:13).

Through All Generations

Your faithfulness continues through all generations.

PSALM 119:90

Thank you for always being faithful, Lord.
I praise you for the promise of your unshakeable love:
    "Though the mountains be shaken and the hills be removed,
    yet my unfailing love for you will not be shaken" (Isaiah 54:10).
"O Sovereign LORD, you are God!
    Your words are trustworthy" (2 Samuel 7:28).
"Your word, O LORD, is eternal" (Psalm 119:89).
It's for future generations that I ask your help, Father, starting with
    my daughter.
When I look at the direction the world is going,
    I'm reminded that "the heart is deceitful above all things
    and beyond cure" (Jeremiah 17:9).
But you are "the LORD, who heals" (Exodus 15:26)!
So, like the parents who brought their children to you,
    I ask you to touch her, Lord Jesus (Matthew 19:13).
She is not as close to you as she needs to be, so I ask you to
    use the situations in her life right now to turn her to you.
Place your people in her path, Father,
    and let her be drawn to them in ways she cannot explain.
Let her see 'coincidences' and understand that they are much more
    than that, because you are at work to capture her heart.
Let her see you moving wherever she goes,
    because "the earth is full" of your "unfailing love" (Psalm 33:5).
I pray that she will no longer be "captive to sin" (Acts 8:23),
    but that she will freely give her heart to you in love.
As I think about her future, Father, I'd also like to pray for the man
    she will one day fall in love with and marry.
I ask that you will be at work in his life as well,
    to save him and show him your way.

I pray that their marriage will be established in your unconditional
love, and that you will be welcomed into their home in every way.

I also pray for any children you would give them, and for grandchildren,
great-grandchildren, and beyond, that "from the lips of children
and infants," you would ordain praise (Matthew 21:16).

I praise you too, Father, because "nothing is too hard for you"
(Jeremiah 32:17).

Because you are faithful from generation to generation,
you are entirely able to answer this prayer,
and I praise you for what you will do!

Everything Is Possible

When the spirit saw Jesus, it immediately threw the boy into a convulsion. He fell to the ground and rolled around, foaming at the mouth. Jesus asked the boy's father, "How long has he been like this?" "From childhood," he answered. "It has often thrown him into fire or water to kill him. But if you can do anything, take pity on us and help us." "'If you can'?" said Jesus. "Everything is possible for him who believes." Immediately the boy's father exclaimed, "I do believe; help me overcome my unbelief!"

MARK 9:20–24

I f you can do anything . . ."

Those words weren't exactly filled with hope. The man who said them to Jesus had tried everything he could think of for his son. Even Jesus' disciples had not been able to help the boy (Mark 9:18).

Jesus is quick to respond: "If you can? . . . Everything is possible for him who believes."

The man jumps hungrily at the thought: "I do believe; help me overcome my unbelief!"

I love that prayer. I've found myself praying it more than once.

When you're the parent of a prodigal, you find your faith challenged in many ways. Sometimes your child challenges what you believe. Other times, you may find yourself struggling when answers to prayer don't come as quickly as you may have hoped.

It's comforting that Jesus didn't rebuke the father for his plea for help with his unbelief. He answered the plea with action. Jesus exercised his spiritual authority and commanded the demon to leave the man's son (Mark 9:25).

In the moment before Jesus spoke to free the man's son, the man's faith hadn't changed. He still had his questions and doubted whether something could be done. He was honest about his struggles and lack of faith, and Jesus met that transparency with kindness.

Even the smallest amount of faith placed in Jesus' hands can move mountains (Matthew 17:20). We need to give not only the situation that weighs so heavily on us to him, but ourselves as well.

Later Jesus' disciples "asked him privately, 'Why couldn't we drive it out?'" Jesus answered, "This kind can come out only by prayer" (Mark 9:28–29). Earlier the disciples had been given "authority over evil spirits" (Mark 6:7). Jesus had sent them out, and they "drove out many demons and anointed many sick people with oil and healed them" (Mark 6:13). So why couldn't they do it this time?

The answer lies in their question. Jesus said that apart from the Father, He could "do nothing" (John 5:30). But the disciples asked: "Why couldn't *we* drive it out?" Their focus was no longer on God's authority and his ability to answer prayer, but on themselves.

Sometimes we pray after we've tried everything else and nothing has seemed to work. Jesus' answer shows that instead we need to make prayer our "first resort" and not our last.[1] Then, we will discover that His power is "made perfect in weakness" (2 Corinthians 12:9).

When by faith we take hold of Jesus, reaching for Him and not just what He can do for us, He *takes hold* of us and lifts us to new places of grace. When we give up control and long for His authority over our lives and the lives of our children, depending on him with new prayerfulness, we discover the hope that "everything is possible for him who believes."

We may have our questions and struggles, but that doesn't change who Jesus is. We can "cast all" our "anxiety on him because he cares for" us (1 Peter 5:7). His words to the struggling father that day are the same to the parents of prodigals today: "Bring the boy to me" (Mark 9:19).

We have to pray with our eyes on God, not on the difficulties.

Oswald Chambers

---

1. Banks, *Lost Art of Praying Together*, 24.

A Larger Lion

Be self-controlled and alert. Your enemy the devil prowls around
like a roaring lion looking for someone to devour.

1 Peter 5:8

I see lion tracks, Lord. Right behind him.
The tracks have been close for a while now. Too close.
My son has been walking in the enemy's territory and he's in danger.
He's being stalked every step he takes, but he doesn't see it.
Help him, Father! "You alone, O Lord,"
　　make him "dwell in safety" (Psalm 4:8).
I pray that you will protect him.
Let him look around the road that he's on and see that it leads nowhere.
I ask that you will turn him around
　　so that his feet no longer "rush into sin" (Proverbs 1:16).
I pray he will "turn from evil and do good,"
　　and "seek peace" with you (Psalm 34:14).
Save him, Father! "Come quickly" to his "rescue" (Psalm 31:2).
Even though the enemy pursues him, I ask that you,
　　"the Lion of tribe of Judah," be swifter still (Revelation 5:5).
Let your love overtake him and protect him every step he takes.
　　"I look for your deliverance, O Lord" (Genesis 49:18).
When the enemy attacks my son, I pray that you "will fight for" him,
　　before his "very eyes" (Deuteronomy 1:30).
I praise you that with you on his side, my son faces a defeated foe.
In the moment that you deliver him, may he hear you speaking to his
　　soul: "I am the Lord, and there is no other; apart from me there is
　　no God. I will strengthen you, though you have not acknowledged
　　me" (Isaiah 45:5).
You say in your Word, Father, that you "will lead the blind by ways
　　they have not known, along unfamiliar paths" you "will guide
　　them;" you "will turn the darkness into light before them and
　　make the rough places smooth" (Isaiah 42:16).

My son needs you to lead him in that way, Lord. Out of the dark
and into the "everlasting light" of your presence
so that his "days of sorrow will end" (Isaiah 60:20).
Those "who walk in the light of your presence" are blessed
(Psalm 89:15), and I want my son to know your blessing!
"Come, Lord Jesus" (Revelation 22:20),
come soon to give my son the grace he needs.
Come into his life in a fresh and powerful way
so that he will surrender his heart to you!

Long in the Land

Children, obey your parents in the Lord, for this is right.
"Honor your father and mother"—which is the first
commandment with a promise—"that it may go well
with you and that you may enjoy long life on the earth."

EPHESIANS 6:1–3

Father, I ask that you will help my daughter to live in such a way
that she may be blessed.

You promise that those who "honor" their "father and mother" *will* be
blessed: it will "go well" with them, and they will "enjoy long life
on the earth."

She's struggling with honoring her parents right now. She thinks that
obedience will lead to a lack of life, instead of one that is better.

Thank you, Father, for the reminder that children are to obey their
parents "in the Lord."

I'm not up to the job of parenting without you!

"Apart from you I have no good thing" (Psalm 16:2).

I praise you that with you I will have all that I need, not only to meet
the challenges of parenting a child who is rebelling, but also to
overcome those challenges.

Your Word gives me this assurance: "Who is it that overcomes the
world? Only he who believes that Jesus is the Son of God"
(1 John 5:5).

I *do* believe in you, Lord. And I thank you that you will get us through
this time.

I pray that you will help my daughter learn to obey even when
it isn't easy.

Help her to see that obedience doesn't mean that she is weak.
Instead, it's a sign of strength of character.

I pray that you will help me to obey you too, Lord.

Obedience to you is the best way to show you that I love you,
   because "this is love for" you: to obey your commands
   (1 John 5:3).
Father, I pray my daughter will also be obedient to you so that she
   "will be blessed" in every way (John 13:17).
Let her love you and follow you!
Give her insight to see that when she walks in the world's ways,
   she is simply conforming to the world and *obeying* it,
   and there is no freedom or originality in that.
Give her grace to understand that "we must obey" you
   "rather than men" (Acts 5:29).
It is only through you that she can discover her true identity,
   all that you uniquely created her to be.
Give me grace as well, Father, for those moments
   when I face my daughter and our wills collide.
I pray "your will be done" (Matthew 26:42) fully and freely in both of
   our lives, because those who do your will, will live in your land
   "forever" (1 John 2:17)!

Sitting in the Courtroom

If you, O LORD, kept a record of sins, O Lord, who could stand?
But with you there is forgiveness; therefore you are feared.

PSALM 130:3–4

He's in trouble, Lord, and he needs your help.
He's up against circumstances so much bigger than he is,
    and he doesn't yet understand the consequences of his actions.
But you love him, and that's my greatest hope.
I hold on to your Word: "But God demonstrates his own love for us in
    this: While we were still sinners, Christ died for us" (Romans 5:8).
You saw this coming and still loved him with the greatest love
    imaginable (John 15:13).
He needs that right now. More than any attorney,
    he needs you to be his "advocate" (Job 16:19).
"Let him turn to the LORD, and he will have mercy on him,
    and to our God, for he will freely pardon" (Isaiah 55:7).
It is your mercy he needs more than anything else.
Not just for what he stands accused of, but for his heart and soul.
Use this, Lord. Use this experience to change his heart
    so that you may "have mercy" on him (Romans 11:32).
Let your kindness lead him "toward repentance" (Romans 2:4).
Let the "godly sorrow" that "brings repentance that leads to salvation
    and leaves no regret" turn his heart entirely to you
    (2 Corinthians 7:10).
Everything in me wants to help him, if only I could.
I know that the best help I can give him is to bring him
    and everything about this situation to you in prayer.
I pray that when we're sitting in the courtroom,
    we will not be afraid because you go with us, and you "will never
    leave" us "nor forsake" us (Deuteronomy 31:6).

I pray that when my son stands before the judge, he will be reminded that "we will all stand before God's judgment seat" (Romans 14:10).

I ask that my son will be respectful and will answer wisely, saying only what you would have him say (see Proverbs 16:1).

I pray that he will "submit himself to the governing authorities" and not rebel in any way (Romans 13:1–2).

I pray as well for the judge, that you will give him "the wisdom that comes from heaven" (James 3:17), and that he will be "God's servant" to do my son "good" (Romans 13:4).

I pray that you will move in the judge's heart to accomplish your purposes, and that mercy will triumph "over judgment" (James 2:13).

I pray all of this in the strong name of Jesus, who stood accused for me (Matthew 27:12) that I may go free (John 8:36).

Should Have, Would Have, Could Have

If only you had paid attention to my commands, your peace would have been like a river, your righteousness like the waves of the sea.

Isaiah 48:18

I know someday she'll have her regrets, Lord.
I'd like to send this prayer on ahead to that time.
One day she will look back on her life and wish she had done things
    differently.
She will regret the difficult things that passed between us and feel
    a hurt in her heart, because of the love you've given us for each
    other.
On that day, Lord, because you are the one "who comforts us in all
    our troubles" (2 Corinthians 1:4), I ask that you quiet her with
    your love.
I pray that she will know your presence and the peace you alone can
    give to those who walk with you as their Lord and Savior.
I ask that you will "speak tenderly" to her,
    and tell her "that her sin has been paid for" (Isaiah 40:2).
Thank you, Father, that we can bring all of our 'should haves, would
    haves, and could haves' to you and find healing and hope.
I pray you will turn her around from the road that leads only to regret
    and draw her heart to you.
I praise you, Lord Jesus, that with you new beginnings are possible
    every day.
With you, we can "press on toward the goal" of heaven and hope
    (Philippians 3:14)!
We need not "long for the months gone by" (Job 29:2),
    because you are always with us.
You even have the future completely under control.
We need not fear tomorrow, because you are already there!
    You hold time in your hands.

Lord, you "wash away all my iniquity and cleanse me from my sin"
(Psalm 51:2).
I pray that your grace will reach my daughter in the same way so
that she can turn her back on the past and look to you with
confidence.
Let her hear you say to her, "Forget the former things; do not dwell on
the past" (Isaiah 43:18).
I pray that she will repent of her sins and know that she is completely
forgiven.
Your Word promises, "If anyone is in Christ, he is a new creation;
the old has gone, the new has come!" (2 Corinthians 5:17).
I pray that she will "be glad and rejoice forever" in what you will
create (Isaiah 65:18), that you may be her joy,
and she will be yours.

Everything She Ever Wanted

The fruit of righteousness will be peace; the effect of righteousness will be quietness and confidence forever.

Isaiah 32:17

If she walks with you, Father, it changes everything.
She will "have peace" in you (John 16:33),
    because you are "our peace" (Ephesians 2:14).
She will have every blessing she needs, because in your grace you
    never take your "eyes off the righteous" (Job 36:7).
What a full and beautiful life you have planned for her, Lord!
Father, I pray she will hear the promptings of your Holy Spirit telling
    her, "In repentance and rest is your salvation,
    in quietness and trust is your strength" (Isaiah 30:15).
Let her repent of her sins and find peace with you!
Because "there is no one righteous, not even one" (Romans 3:10),
    I pray for the righteousness only you can give, which is
    "righteousness, peace and joy in the Holy Spirit" (Romans 14:17).
Clothe her "with garments of salvation" (Isaiah 61:10),
    because "all our righteous acts are like filthy rags" (Isaiah 64:6).
If she asks you for wisdom, you "give freely to all without finding
    fault!" (James 1:5).
I pray that she will ask and "will receive"
    so that her "joy will be complete" (John 16:24).
You are complete joy, Lord! Please help her to make that discovery.
Then she will find everything she ever wanted in all that you are.
I pray that she will come to "the full measure of the blessing of
    Christ" (Romans 15:29) and become a blessing to others!
If she comes to you and remains in you, she will "bear much fruit"
    (John 15:5).
I also ask that she will be fruitful by pointing others to you.
May she "bear fruit—fruit that will last" (John 15:16),
    and "still bear fruit in old age" (Psalm 92:14).

Let her share the story of what you have done for her with confidence to all who will listen!

But first, let her discover your "incomparably great power for us who believe" (Ephesians 1:19).

O Father, let today be the day!

In All Things, God

And we know that in all things God works for the good of those who love him, who have been called according to his purpose.

ROMANS 8:28

It amazes me, Father, how you waste nothing.
You are sovereign over every single experience of life.
You use it all—the happy times and the heartbreaking ones—to bring
    good that you alone can give.
As I look back on my life with my child, Lord,
    I think of how I imagined it very differently.
I didn't expect the challenges we've faced together,
    and I know that she doesn't bear responsibility for all of them.
I know I've made mistakes too, Lord.
Thank you for your mercy and grace that meet us both right
    where we are.
She needs it to open her eyes and turn her "darkness to light"
    (Acts 26:18).
I need it to remind me of your "everlasting love" (Jeremiah 31:3),
    and that even though I stumble, I "will not fall,"
        because you hold me up with your hand (Psalm 37:24).
I praise you, Lord, for the unexpected mercies along the way—
    good things that I didn't expect that were clearly from your hand.
How true it is that your "compassions never fail.
    They are new every morning" (Lamentations 3:22–23).
Thank you for your fresh mercy that meets us every day, Father!
Thank you for "the incomparable riches" of your grace that you want to
    show us in your "kindness to us in Christ Jesus" (Ephesians 2:7).
There are good days ahead as we turn to you. Help us to do it, Lord!
Your Word promises that "he who fears the LORD has a secure fortress,
    and for his children it will be a refuge" (Proverbs 14:26).
My child needs your refuge, Lord, and "the shelter of your presence"
    to keep her safe (Psalm 31:20).

"You are forgiving and good, O Lord, abounding in love
to all who call to you" (Psalm 86:5).
I call on you, Father, because "no one can fathom"
your greatness (Psalm 145:3).
I call on you, Lord Jesus, because you "have overcome the world"
(John 16:33).
I call on you, Holy Spirit, because you search
"even the deep things of God" (1 Corinthians 2:10).
You alone, Lord, can bring us safely through the storm.
How faithful you are to your promises,
and how loving you are to us (Psalm 145:13)!
I stand on your Word today: "I sought the LORD, and he answered me;
he delivered me from all my fears" (Psalm 34:4).
I praise you that you are a God who "richly blesses all who call" on
you (Romans 10:12)!

River of Delights

*How priceless is your unfailing love! Both high and low among men
find refuge in the shadow of your wings. They feast on the abundance
of your house; you give them drink from your river of delights.*

PSALM 36:8

A "river of delights." What a beautiful thought!
Show my son the way to that river, Lord.
Let him dive in headfirst and discover "how wide and long and
    high and deep is the love of Christ" (Ephesians 3:18)!
I can see him splashing around in it, his face a picture of joy.
Let him drink of its sweet, refreshing water
    and "never thirst" again (John 4:14).
I pray that you will satisfy every longing of his soul.
You are the true source of every delight,
    "the spring of living water" (Jeremiah 17:13).
"Every good and perfect gift" comes from you (James 1:17)!
You say in your Word, "Whoever is thirsty, let him come;
    and whoever wishes, let him take the free gift of the water of life"
    (Revelation 22:17).
You promise that "to him who is thirsty" you "will give to drink
    without cost from the spring of the water of life" (Revelation 21:6).
He is thirsty, Lord. But right now he doesn't understand that only you
    can quench his thirst.
I ask that he will understand, and the sooner, the better.
Good Shepherd, I ask you to lead my son to the clear,
    "quiet waters" of your peace, and there restore his soul
    (Psalm 23:2–3).
He's swum in the devil's sewage long enough.
"Wash" him, and he "will be clean" (Psalm 51:7).
Just as you are "able to guard what I have entrusted" to you
    (2 Timothy 1:12), grab him by the hand and pull him up from the
    world's deadly and filthy undertow.

Save him, Lord! Breathe into him the breath of eternal life.

Show him the beautiful, pure person you intend him to be,
> filled with your Spirit and with your love.

May your "righteousness" roll on "like a never-failing stream," Savior
> (Amos 5:24)!

I praise you for "the river of the water of life, as clear as crystal,
> flowing from the throne of God and of the Lamb"
> (Revelation 22:1).

Let him be lifted by your water of life and carried to new places of
> grace.

Then he will show others the way to the river too, because "streams
> of living water will flow from within him" (John 7:38).

And together we'll swim in your joy forever!

God's Timing

Jesus told the synagogue ruler, "Don't be afraid; just believe."

MARK 5:36

Sometimes God doesn't give us what we're asking for so that he can give us what we really want.

That's what happened to Monica. For more than nine years, she prayed for her son Augustine to come to Christ. She prayed with such passion that a bishop in their city told her, "It is not possible that the son of these tears should perish."[1]

But as Monica prayed, her son wandered further and further from God. When she learned that he wanted to leave their home in North Africa to sail to Rome, the center of vice and corruption in her time, she became distraught and followed him all the way to the harbor where the ship was waiting.

Then he tricked her.

Augustine told her he could not leave until a friend was ready to sail. He suggested she get some rest that night at a chapel beside the harbor. While she was sleeping, he left. She looked out on the harbor the next morning to discover that the ship had sailed and her son with it, *the very thing she was praying would not happen.*

But it was in Rome that Augustine would give his heart to God. His life would be transformed forever, and God would use Augustine's faith to inspire generations to believe in Jesus.

Augustine later recalled the evening he left his mother in his book *Confessions*: "The wind blew and swelled our sails, and withdrew the shore from our sight; and she on the morrow was there, frantic with sorrow, and with complaints and groans filled Thine

---

1. Augustine, *Confessions*, 5.8, available at http://www.ccel.org/ccel/augustine/confess.vi.viii.html.

ears, Who didst then disregard them." He concludes insightfully, "Thou, in the depth of Thy counsels and hearing the main point of her desire, regardest not what she then asked, that Thou mightest make me what she ever asked."[2]

When the very thing you're praying won't happen *does*, it's easy to become discouraged.

I have to wonder how Jairus felt. He came to Jesus and "fell at his feet and pleaded earnestly with him, 'My little daughter is dying. Please come and put your hands on her so that she will be healed and live.'" While they were on the way to Jairus's home, a woman who was chronically ill pressed through the crowd and touched Jesus. "At once Jesus realized that power had gone out from him. He turned around in the crowd and asked, 'Who touched my clothes?'"

If I were Jairus, I would be thinking, 'My daughter is *dying*, and you're stopping in a *crowd* to ask a question like that?' Even the disciples wondered aloud, "You see the people crowding against you . . . yet you can ask, 'Who touched me?'"

Jesus not only stopped, He *kept waiting.* "Jesus kept looking around to see who had done it. Then the woman, knowing what had happened to her, came and fell at his feet and, trembling with fear, told him the whole truth."

For Jairus, this meant more delays. Then men from his house showed up and they were hardly compassionate: "'Your daughter is dead,' they said. 'Why bother the teacher any more?'"

Jesus ignored them. He told Jairus, "Don't be afraid; just believe."

You know how the story ends. Jesus went to Jairus's house, and the mourners laughed at Him. He threw them out and brought the girl back to life (Mark 5:22–43).

Praying for a prodigal will stretch your faith. What can help in the especially difficult times is to remember that God's timing is rarely our own. Things may seem to go from bad to worse, but He has complete authority over the situation. When it seems like hope is lost, it only means God isn't finished yet.

Sometimes we wonder why we keep praying. In those times, it's good to remember that the heartless and laughing voice of doubt never has the last word. That word belongs to God. Jesus moves at

---

2. Ibid., 5.8.

His own pace, and He is never late. His advice to a worried parent long ago still speaks to us today: "Don't be afraid; just believe."

God is faithful, and He will answer our prayers in His perfect timing and wisdom. His Word reminds us that His ways and thoughts are "higher" than our own (Isaiah 55:9). He is never flustered or delayed, and nothing can stop Him from carrying out His purposes. Though we may not be able to see Him coming, that doesn't mean that He isn't about to show up in a life-giving way that changes everything for the better. Just around the corner, we may bump into the grace God intended all along.

The joyful discovery Jairus and Monica made is ours to make as well.

Hope isn't lost. It is only taking another way.

When I am dealing with an all-powerful, all-knowing God,
I, as a mere mortal, must offer my petitions not only with
persistence but also with patience. Someday I'll know why.

Ruth Bell Graham

Those Who Are with Us

"Don't be afraid," the prophet answered. "Those who are
with us are more than those who are with them." And Elisha
prayed, "O LORD, open his eyes so he may see." Then the
LORD opened the servant's eyes, and he looked and saw the
hills full of horses and chariots of fire all around Elisha.

2 KINGS 6:16–17

When I try to wrap my mind around all that you are, Lord,
    I am simply astounded.
Your Word tells me of "thousands upon thousands of angels in joyful
    assembly" around you (Hebrews 12:22).
You said of our children that "their angels in heaven always see"
    the Father's face (Matthew 18:10).
How wonderful you are, Lord!
"What is man, that you are mindful of him?" (Psalm 8:4).
You are "majestic in holiness, awesome in glory, working wonders"
    (Exodus 15:11).
It helps to keep that in mind. Sometimes it seems like my child and I
    are up against things that seem so much bigger than we.
The times that we live in, the culture, the media—all of these things
    affect our lives in ways beyond our control.
But I praise you that they are not beyond yours!
I thank you that one day "every knee should bow, in heaven and on
    earth . . . and every tongue confess that Jesus Christ is Lord"
    (Philippians 2:10).
You are Lord over every challenge we face, and all of history is heading
    in your direction, "Judge of all the earth" (Genesis 18:25)!
Lord Jesus, I thank you that "trouble or hardship or persecution or
    famine or nakedness or danger or sword" shall not "separate us"
    from your love (Romans 8:35).
My son needs your love, and he needs to know you.

Right now he is impressed with "the ways of this world" (Ephesians 2:2), which are "passing away" (1 Corinthians 7:31).

"O Lord, open his eyes so he may see."

Just as you opened the eyes of Elisha's servant, I pray that you will help my son to see that "there is none like you" (Psalm 86:8).

Give him grace to understand that he wants to be on your side, because "those who are with us are more than those who are with them."

One day, you will bring all of history to a close.

I pray we will both be ready on the day that you return, Lord Jesus!

Then we will look "forward to a new heaven and a new earth, the home of righteousness" (2 Peter 3:13), where "the earth will be full of the knowledge of the Lord, as the waters cover the sea" (Isaiah 11:9).

For Strength to Love

Who shall separate us from the love of Christ?
Shall trouble or hardship or persecution or
famine or nakedness or danger or sword?

ROMANS 8:35

"I love you, O LORD, my strength" (Psalm 18:1).
I love you because you've "freely given" me your grace (Ephesians 1:6).
You loved me even before "the creation of the world" (Ephesians 1:4).
When I was completely lost and "dead in transgressions,"
    you loved me and gave me life (Ephesians 2:4–5).
You are love, Lord (1 John 4:16)! "Your love is better than life"
    (Psalm 63:3).
Your "love compels" me (2 Corinthians 5:14).
    I want to live in your love, Lord.
Over every virtue I want to "put on love" (Colossians 3:14).
I want to live with faith and hope and love,
    "but the greatest of these is love" (1 Corinthians 13:13).
"Love never fails" (1 Corinthians 13:8).
I want others to sense your love in me before I even say a word.
Especially my son.
My son is a gift and blessing from you. I love him so much, Father!
But as much as I love him, you love him even more.
Your love is perfect! Your love is "from everlasting to everlasting"
    (Psalm 103:17).
He needs your love so much.
Love through me, Lord! Let your love flow through me to draw
    him to you.
I know what love is because you've showed it to me through the
    way you "laid down" your life and loved me so sacrificially
    (1 John 3:16).
Father, give me grace to love like you do.
I ask for the strength to love him when it isn't easy.

Help me to love him enough to be patient with him,
   because "love is patient" (1 Corinthians 13:4).
Help me to speak "the truth in love" (Ephesians 4:15)
   and share your Word with him.
When he does something wrong, help me to love him enough to
   discipline him "because the Lord disciplines those he loves"
   (Hebrews 12:6).
When he does something right, let me be the first to praise him,
   because love "rejoices with the truth" (1 Corinthians 13:6).
Father, you are "slow to anger, abounding in love
   and forgiving sin and rebellion" (Numbers 14:18).
I want to love him like that, with a love that "always protects, always
   trusts, always hopes, always perseveres" (1 Corinthians 13:7).
I choose to love, Father, just as you chose to love me.
Fill me afresh with your Spirit, so that I can
   "do everything in love" (1 Corinthians 16:14).
Make my love "increase and overflow," Lord (1 Thessalonians 3:12),
   for you and for my son, that he may one day praise you for it and
   love you with all his heart, soul, mind, and strength (Mark 12:30).

Hiding Place

*You are my hiding place; you will protect me from trouble
and surround me with songs of deliverance.*

PSALM 32:7

I remember when we used to play hide-and-seek. We had so
much fun!
She used to love to be found. I'd pick her up in my arms,
hold her close, and we'd both laugh together.
I have that picture in my mind of you, Lord.
You took children in your arms and "blessed them" (Mark 10:16).
I ask that you do that for my daughter once again.
You are the Good Shepherd, who "gathers the lambs in his arms
and carries them close to his heart" (Isaiah 40:11).
She needs your touch, Lord (Luke 18:15).
She needs you to take her by the hand and lead her "in paths of
righteousness" for your name's sake (Psalm 23:3).
When she was little, she would try to hide by covering her eyes,
as if that were enough.
That's not unlike what she's trying to do now, Father,
even though you see her "every step" (Job 34:21).
I remember the times that I've tried to hide from you, but in your
kindness you made me understand: "Where can I go from your
Spirit? Where can I flee from your presence?" (Psalm 139:7).
Nothing in all creation is hidden from your sight (Hebrews 4:13).
I pray that you will open her eyes that she "may know the hope"
to which you have called her (Ephesians 1:18).
I pray that she will no longer run *from* you, but run *to* you,
because you have set her heart free (Psalm 119:32).
I pray that you will be her "hiding place," Father.
Then you will protect her from trouble and surround her with "songs
of deliverance" (Psalm 32:7), just as you have me.

May she "take refuge" under your wings (Ruth 2:12)
  and hear the still, small voice of your Spirit in a "gentle whisper"
  telling her she is loved (1 Kings 19:12).
"Make your face shine upon" her, dear Lord,
  to restore her and save her in every way (Psalm 80:3).
Then she will "find delight in the Almighty" and lift her face to you
  (Job 22:26). Her face will shine with your light and your love,
  because those who look to you are "radiant; their faces are never
  covered with shame" (Psalm 34:5).

Always There

And surely I am with you always, to the very end of the age.

Matthew 28:20

'He was always there for me' is one of the best things that can be said
about a parent.
I pray that my daughter will one day say that about me, Father.
I thank you and praise you that I can say that about you!
Wherever I go, your wonderful Spirit goes with me:
"If I go up to the heavens, you are there;
if I make my bed in the depths, you are there" (Psalm 139:8).
I am never alone. You draw close to me in your kindness,
and bless me with "your presence forever" (Psalm 41:12).
If I went to the other side of the world or even the deepest region of
space, "even there your hand will guide me, your right hand will
hold me fast" (Psalm 139:10).
What could matter more than simply being with you?
What could I possibly need "besides you" (Psalm 73:25)?
There is "one thing I ask" of you, Lord (Psalm 27:4).
As blessed as I am to know that you are with me always and that I will
one day be with you, I long for my child to love you too.
Your Word says that "the children of your servants will live in your
presence; their descendants will be established before you"
(Psalm 102:28).
"O Lord, truly I am your servant" (Psalm 116:16)
because of your kindness and grace!
I pray that my daughter will live in your presence in heaven and in the
kingdom to come by first coming to faith in you on this earth.
May she know in her heart that our love for her, strong as it is,
pales in comparison with yours!
All love comes from you. Your Word even says, "Though my father
and mother forsake me," you "will receive me" (Psalm 27:10)!
Thank you for holding out your arms for her, Lord Jesus.

May there be no doubt that she has received you,
    so that you may receive her forever.
"To all who received" you, "to those who believed in" your name,
    you "gave the right to become children of God" (John 1:12).
I pray that right will be hers, Father, and I give her to you again today.
She is my child, but I want her to be yours as well, just as you made
    me your child through your incredible mercy in Jesus.

He Is Yours, and So Am I

"I am the Lord's servant," Mary answered. "May it be
to me as you have said." Then the angel left her.

Luke 1:38

Mary's response was amazing, Father.
After the angel told her news that would turn her life upside down,
    she simply said, "I am the Lord's servant."
She didn't ask, 'What will Joseph say when he discovers I'm pregnant?'
    Or, 'What will people think?'
She just gave herself and her son to you.
I want to do the same thing, Father.
I know that he is better off in your hands than mine.
But it isn't easy. He is *my* son, but he is also *your gift.*
Because I love him, I want to protect him.
    I want to keep him from pain and harm.
The thought of giving him up in any way goes straight to my soul.
I remember what Simeon told Mary:
    "A sword will pierce your own soul too" (Luke 2:35).
I can't imagine what Mary went through, seeing her own son crucified.
But *you* went through the same thing, Father! He was *your* son too.
That is the very thing that gives me hope and lets me know that it's
    safe to give my son to you: "He who did not spare his own Son,
    but gave him up for us all—how will he not also, along with him,
    graciously give us all things?" (Romans 8:32).
Forgive me for being possessive, Lord.
How can I not give you my son when you have given yours to me?
So I pray with your Son, my Savior,
    "Not my will, but yours be done," Father (Luke 22:42).
I place my son in your hands. He needs you more than anything else.
Because you "graciously give us all things" (Romans 8:32), I ask that
    you give him grace to receive you so that he may "be filled to the
    measure of all the fullness of God" (Ephesians 3:19).

I ask that he will "consider everything a loss compared to the surpassing greatness of knowing Christ Jesus" (Philippians 3:8).

You said it yourself, Lord: "What good is it for a man to gain the whole world, yet forfeit his soul?" (Mark 8:36).

Thank you, Father, for the peace that comes when I bow not just my head, but my heart to you as well.

In my heart, I "set apart Christ as Lord" (1 Peter 3:15), and thank you for the blessing that will come.

I Believe

We live by faith, not by sight.

2 CORINTHIANS 5:7

I believe, Father.

I believe that you want me to pray for my child because my prayers
will make a profound difference for good in her life.

I believe that you gave her to me for a reason that has more to do with
your vision for her eternity than my wishes for her on this earth.

I believe that you want me to be "wrestling in prayer" for her
(Colossians 4:12) so that through prayer, things will change for
the better.

No matter what the situation looks like now or what other people may
say, no matter what conventional, earthly wisdom may forecast
for her future, I will believe *you.*

I will seek you above all others,
because "you have the words of eternal life" (John 6:68).

I will "live by faith, not by sight" and always hold on to hope.

"Hope does not disappoint us," because you have poured out your
"love into our hearts by the Holy Spirit," whom you have given us
(Romans 5:5).

Like Jacob wrestling, "I will not let you go unless you bless me"
(Genesis 32:26), and I praise you that you will never let me go,
because you have said, "Never will I leave you; never will I
forsake you" (Hebrews 13:5).

I will persevere for my daughter with prayer after prayer until she
realizes how much you love her.

I want my daughter to love you, Lord,
and I believe that one day she will—fully, freely, joyfully.

I believe, Lord, because your Word tells me that "without faith it
is impossible to please" you, because anyone who comes to
you must believe that you exist and that you reward those who
earnestly seek you (Hebrews 11:6).

I believe you will reward me as I seek you with all of my heart,
   and you will bless my daughter as she turns to you.
I believe that the future you have in store for her is beautiful,
   filled with "grace and peace" (1 Peter 1:2).
I believe because in your great mercy you have given me
   "new birth into a living hope through the resurrection of Jesus
   Christ from the dead" (1 Peter 1:3).
Because you are the "hope of glory" (Colossians 1:27), Jesus, and you
   are in me, my hope will live always: today, tomorrow,
   and forevermore!

CONCLUSION

Prayer moves the hand that moves the world.

E. M. BOUNDS

William didn't have time for his mother's Christian faith. Though she spoke with him frequently about Jesus and he often caught her praying for his salvation, he kept going his own way.

Before she died, she gave him a Bible.

He sold it when he needed some extra cash.

Still, William was what you might call a "successful" prodigal. He graduated from medical school and began working as a physician in a hospital.

One day, a man was brought in who had been in a serious accident on the job. William did his best to help him, but it was clear that the man would soon die from his injuries. William broke the news to him as best he could.

The man had two requests. He asked to see his landlady so he could pay his rent, and he requested she bring him his Bible.

In the days that followed, he kept the Bible close. He read it as long as he could. When he no longer had the strength to hold it, he kept it under his covers. He died a short time later.

A nurse was cleaning his room after his death and found the Bible. "What shall we do with this?" she asked William, handing it to him.

William's own words recount what happened next:

> I took the Bible and—could I trust my eyes? It was my own Bible! The Bible which my mother had given me when I left my parents' home, and which later, when short of money, I sold for a small amount. My name was still in it, written in my mother's hand . . .
>
> With a deep sense of shame I looked upon . . . the precious book. It had given comfort and refreshing to the unfortunate man in his last hours. It had been a guide to him

into eternal life, so that he had been enabled to die in peace and happiness. And this Book, the last gift of my mother, I had actually sold for a ridiculous price . . .

Be it sufficient to say that the regained possession of my Bible was the cause of my conversion.[1]

William's mother never saw her prayers for her son answered on earth, but she did see them answered in heaven. Through her prayers and faith, God used her to reach her son years after her life in this world was over. She placed her trust in him, and he showed himself faithful. After all, He is the One who promised, "In this world you will have trouble. But take heart! I have overcome the world" (John 16:33).

"Take heart!" We need to hear those words from Jesus again and again.

Jesus said them often.

As he bent over a young man stricken with paralysis, he told him, "Take heart, son . . ." (Matthew 9:2).

When a chronically ill woman reached out to touch his coat, he whispered, "Take heart, daughter . . ." (Matthew 9:22).

God hears our prayers for our prodigal sons and daughters and *will* show himself faithful. Even when the challenges seem insurmountable, we can *take heart* because He holds the world in His hands. Even when the answers to our prayers seem long in coming, they are on the way.

That brings us back to William.

Dr. William P. Mackay eventually left medicine and became a minister. God used him to inspire many through his books and hymns. His best known hymn, "Revive Us Again," shows a passionate and faithful heart filled with a contagious love for his Maker:

We praise Thee, O God, for Thy Spirit of light,
Who has shown us our Savior and scattered our night.
Hallelujah! Thine the glory! Hallelujah! Amen!
Hallelujah! Thine the glory! Revive us again!

I have a feeling that when he wrote those words, his mother must have been smiling.

---

1. Quoted in Morgan, *Then Sings My Soul*, 147.

Augustine, Aurelius. *The Confessions of St. Augustine.* Translated by Edward B. Pusey. Oak Harbor, WA: Logos Research Systems, Inc., 1999. Available at Christian Classics Ethereal Library, http://www .ccel.org/ccel/augustine/confess.i.html.

Banks, James. *The Lost Art of Praying Together.* Grand Rapids: Discovery House, 2009.

Bounds, Edward McKendree. *The Complete Works of E. M. Bounds on Prayer.* Grand Rapids: Baker, 1990.

Chambers, Oswald. *Prayer, A Holy Occupation.* Grand Rapids: Discovery House, 1992.

Chesteron, Gilbert Keith. *Orthodoxy.* Garden City, NY: Image Books, 1959.

Cymbala, Jim. *Fresh Faith.* Grand Rapids: Zondervan, 1999.

————. *Fresh Wind, Fresh Fire.* Grand Rapids: Zondervan, 1997.

Faber, Frederick William. *Growth in Holiness.* Baltimore: John Murphy and Company, 1855.

Graham, Ruth Bell. *Prodigals and Those Who Love Them.* Grand Rapids: Baker, 1999.

Morgan, Robert J. *Moments for Families with Prodigals.* Colorado Springs, CO: Navpress, 2003.

————. *Then Sings My Soul.* Nashville: Thomas Nelson, 2003.

Newton, John, and William Cowper. *Olney Hymns.* London: W. Oliver, 1797.

Pascal, Blaise. *Pensees.* Translated by W. F. Trotter. Christian Classics Ethereal Library, http://www.ccel.org/ccel/pascal/pensees.i.html.

Prime, Samuel. *The Power of Prayer.* Edinburgh, Scotland: The Banner of Truth Trust, 1991.

Spurgeon, Charles Haddon. *The C. H. Spurgeon Collection.* Rio, WI: Ages Software, 1998–2001.

NOTE TO THE READER

The publisher invites you to share your response to the message of this book by writing Discovery House, P.O. Box 3566, Grand Rapids, MI 49501, U.S.A. For information about other Discovery House books, music, or DVDs, contact us at the same address or call 1-800-653-8333. Find us on at dhp.org or send e-mail to books@dhp.org.

James would love to come encourage your church or group in prayer (especially in praying for prodigals). For more information about hosting an event with James, please contact him at JamesBanks.org.